The Power Behind
Aston Martin

Geoff Courtney
Roger Stowers

Oxford Illustrated Press

Filmset by Oxprint Limited, Oxford
Printed by B. H. Blackwell, Oxford
Bound by R. J. Acford Limited, Chichester

ISBN 0 902280 58 9

The Oxford Illustrated Press Limited,
Shelley Close, Headington, Oxford

Contents

To Brigitte and Andrea

Acknowledgement is gratefully
accorded to Aston Martin
Lagonda (1975) Limited for
ready access to post-war records
which have helped considerably
with photographic research.
This applies also to the Aston
Martin Owners Club for
permission to use the
photograph (Atom) on page
29, but particularly for their
Register, without which no
Member's library is complete.
Much information has been
assimilated from it over the
years of the photographer's
membership but it has been
invaluable as an aid to detail
accuracy. Also to *Auto-
car* for permission to reproduce
the photograph of the 1½-litre
saloon.

Foreword

I must make a confession. I am not one of that understandable and dedicated group of people universally known as "Aston Martin enthusiasts". Not because of any faults with this admirable marque, I hasten to add. Simply because a car is, to me, more a means of transport than a subject for adulation and idolatry. You don't have to fall hopelessly in love with an actress to enjoy watching her on the big screen, nor do you have to study Wisden daily to appreciate a cricket match. So it is with cars. I enjoy driving, I appreciate the finer qualities of certain makes above others, and I find pleasure in looking at the work of a good stylist. Yet becoming obsessed with a particular breed, whatever its merits and charisma, is failing to acknowledge its very raison d'etre. Surely the car most to be admired is one which does what it was built for despite the way it is, or is not, looked after? To me, a breakdown is a nuisance and an inconvenience. To an enthusiast it is a challenge. There is a very narrow divide between pride and obsession.

The difference in attitudes between myself and the 'enthusiast' is no better illustrated than the opinion I hold of a certain Aston Martin, and that held by Roger Stowers, who is responsible for every photograph in this book and who is an Aston Martin man right down to his bed socks. The car in question started life as a DB4 in the early Sixties, but within a few years had grafted on to it a DB5 front and DB6 back. To me, it is probably the prettiest car ever to carry the Aston Martin badge, with perfect proportions and a mixture of masculine agressiveness and delicate refinement. I even like the very non-standard colour. To Roger it is an abomination, a bastardisation for which he wouldn't give garage room. It is repulsive to his purist eyes; a pretender to a throne it should not even be allowed to look at. It is unique, and Roger is grateful for that. He is glad the idea didn't catch on.

Yet in my opening remark I said it was understandable why anyone should become an Aston Martin enthusiast. Such an apparent contradiction of opinions demands an explanation. I have been connected with cars all my life; my father was an oil company executive, and since leaving school my career has always come into contact with them. I have given talks about cars, written about them, broadcast about them, bought them and sold them. Yet no manufacturer has ever taken precedence over any other in my thoughts—until Aston Martin came along.

Introduction

My introduction to the world of Aston Martin was about ten years ago, when I was motoring correspondent for a couple of evening newspapers not far from the Newport Pagnell factory. I road-tested in my columns the DB6 and, in the ensuing decade, reported on the V8 in both manual and automatic form. With this period being a fairly traumatic one for the company, I also wrote a number of stories about the fluctuating fortunes of this world-famous name. I did not know it, but the gravitational pull of that Buckinghamshire firm had begun to suck me to its centre.

When Aston Martin's troubles became public in the latter part of 1974, reaction was incredible. It was as if the very fabric of British life was being threatened, as if a war had been declared on the nation. If the Greater London Council had announced plans to demolish Buckingham Palace, I am convinced it would have gone unheeded beneath the avalanche of hysteria directed up the M1. The company was subsequently saved, but my curiosity had been aroused to an insatiable extent. What in God's name did Aston Martin possess which reduced businessmen to near-panic, had women reading the newspapers for the latest bulletins on the patient, and caused children to write to the factory offering their savings to help the rescue? In the past two years, since becoming responsible for the firm's press and public relations affairs, I think I have found the answers.

To begin with, Aston Martin had never, until latterly been seriously run as a motor manufacturer with an accent on profits. It was more a club and a way of life. Still today the factory, situated in a rather haphazard fashion on the west side of Newport Pagnell, sets the scene by shunning the impersonal corridors and soulless offices associated with many of its contemporaries. Instead, the managing director and other administrative staff share an old detached house, the large service area has the aura of a cathedral which commands reverance from all who step inside by its high sweeping roof and uncanny quietness, and the production side is populated by craftsmen who, by every rule in an accountant's book, should have faced their demise with the coming of the industrial revolution.

Customers, both real and potential, are actively encouraged to visit the factory, to talk to the management and to stroll through the production area at a leisurely pace. There is no room for the furious bustle normally associated with twentieth-century business life. At least, not on the surface. Once a car is ordered, the expectant owner can follow the three-month pregnancy by visiting the factory as often as he likes, chat to the men—and women—who will be responsible for the birth, and soak up the atmosphere which Aston Martin feel is a vital part of fathering one of their products. It is no use, however, having the best doorman in town, and creating the most attractive of surroundings, if the facilities offered inside are second rate. The Aston Martin, as a car, must live up to the standard set by Aston Martin, the company. This is where the tangible is replaced by the intangible, where the almost indefinable attraction of the Aston Martin motor car takes over.

Purchasing an Aston Martin is like buying a friend, a companion who will always be there but who is intelligent enough to bring you down to earth if the need arises. It is also a friend with character and a soul of its own. It is of the highest breeding, very sophisticated and possessing a taste for the good things of life. How, may you ask, can an amalgamation of alloy, steel, cowhides and a variety of other man-made and natural materials possess character and breeding? How indeed. In the 1960s Aston Martin built the revered six-cylinder DB series of two-door saloons and convertibles, while the Seventies saw the emergence of the even higher-performance V8 grand tourer. That latter model, which carried the fortunes of the company in recent years while the advanced four-door Lagonda went through nasty growing pains, is to some—but certainly not to all—the epitome of Aston Martin motoring, It sums up on four massive wheels what owning one of these cars is all about. It is a friend because it gives one a sense of pride, of well-being. It is one of the few remaining hand-assembled cars in the world, and looks and feels like it. Aston Martin are the bespoke tailors of the motor industry. Intelligence is revealed by the way it overcomes any stupidity by the person behind the wheel. Dive into a bend too fast for your own ability or for the prevailing conditions, and the V8 will get you out of trouble. It will slap your wrists, but won't let you break your neck. Not for nothing has it been called 'the most forgiving car in the world.'

Breeding is something this car possesses in abundance. It has a pedigree which contains victory in the World Sports Car Championship—and that to motoring is what a Cruft's top prize is to the canine world. Like an actress whose genuine beauty needs no camouflage courtesy of Goya or Revlon, the V8 is devoid of extraneous make-up. There may be a slight use of the powder-puff to enhance what is naturally there, but no heavy hand is needed. An Aston Martin looks, and is, the part. Yet perhaps its most endearing factor is the way miles are eaten up with such consummate, almost disdainful, ease. There is enough power to restore previous speeds after obstacles are gone, and it has a long-legged stride which would gladden the heart of a racehorse trainer. Without so much as a deep breath, it will gallop at the merest hint of request from the driver, and long journeys become a joy instead of a chore. Many high-performance cars like to let you know how hard they are working on your behalf, and remind you of your demands with a cacophony more reminiscent of a junior school band at practice than a form of expensive transportation. Such a crude thought would never occur to an Aston Martin.

I know of one owner who deserted the V8 cause after owning a string of the cars, and to the astonishment of his family drove home in another make. For two months he swears neither of his sons spoke to him, and such was the atmosphere that eventually he conceded defeat. He acknowledges he made a mistake, he is now back in the V8 fold, and harmony is restored at home. I wonder if there is any other make of car which could disunite a family. Somehow I doubt it.

But what of the future? Can a company who hand assemble six cars a week survive in today's fierce, cruel and often unfair world? Are there still enough people willing to pay for such a product, particularly with the volume producers improving their standards with each model change? I think the answers are yes, and there are. Motoring today is becoming more and more a chore, a necessary evil between business appointments, visits to relatives or just slogging to and from work. Ever-restrictive regulations and the wants of the public have ensured rivals are becoming increasingly similar, and within years most of us will be driving around in anonymously-styled boxes which have as much individualism as a bee in a hive. To some of us that will not be the cause of concern, but to others it will be just further proof that progress can mean a backward step. There will always be individuals who have no desire to become part of the herd, and can afford to graze in different pastures.

While Aston Martin refuse to join the stampede of the masses, while they place quality, craftsmanship and ultra-safe performance above all else, while they continually acknowledge that a pedigree is only as good as the last entries made in it, and while they are run by astute management, they will survive. If they become greedy, lower their standards or rest on their laurels they would be at the top of the slippery slope to oblivion—a slope which has claimed many a victim in the specialist car world. That slope is always waiting, ever eager to grab another prize, another notch in its belt. I can't see the name of Aston Martin there somehow.

The aim of Roger and I in this book is to illustrate the love, devotion, dedication and tears which have helped to make Aston Martin what it is today. It is not a book for the man who would rather read about carburettors than characters, or halfshafts than human beings. Tradition is not formed by things, but people. History is best recounted by those who made it, rather than by those who have studied it, so the following chapters set out the history story of Aston Martin through the eyes of people involved with the marque almost from the beginning.

It ends with the thoughts of a man who is at present on his seventh Aston Martin. That is what you call an enthusiast.

1 Augustus Bertelli

Augustus Cesare Bertelli is as capable of holding the stage today as he was at the Aston Martin factory fifty years ago. His bright eyes belie his eighty-eight years, and his mind is just as searching and his curiosity as active as when he was a young engineer. He reminisces in a stop-go fashion. His answer to a question may be instant, it may be delayed. He may pause for breath at the end of a sentence while in full flood, but meet a drought which dries him up for perhaps five or more seconds. His eyes then deepen in concentration, he shuts out the modern world and reverts to the old.

His wife Vera will occasionally prompt, for sometimes he talks of the 1930s when he means the 1920s, or of a factory in London when he means the Midlands. Dates and places become a blur when you have seen, heard and done as much as Augustus Bertelli.

Yet his alertness is no better shown than by his adaptability to being interviewed. It was, he said, something of an unusual experience, and he apologised before we started in anticipation of his making my job unnecessarily difficult. He needn't have bothered, for frequently he paused to give my writing time to catch up with his speaking, and I managed to note everything far easier than most of the numerous interviews I had previously handled.

This, then, is the story of Bertelli by Bertelli. The story of a man who many regard as the Father of Aston Martin, of a man who by brilliance, determination and guts steered the company through what was arguably its most difficult period, yet who, with a faithful few, gave to the world such masterpieces as the International and Le Mans. These were cars which provided the foundation of quality, craftsmanship and performance which is carried on today, half a

1

century later. The businessmen who run the modern Aston Martin company, and the customers who buy their wares, owe much to Bert, as he is universally known.

Born in the north Italian town of Genoa in 1890, Bert and his family moved to Cardiff four years later, and the formative years spent there are still evident in the whiff of a Welsh accent which sometimes over-rides his essentially English speech. Genoa to Cardiff is an unlikely immigrant route but it was, explains Bert, politically expedient.

'The old man was a Socialist, and in those days that was looked upon in the same way as Bolsheviks are regarded today. Our move was a case of political exile. He was marvellous at making speeches and was able to hold quite an audience, but he didn't really have a profession—I used to regard him as an intellectual.'

With Wales regarding Rugby as its national sport, Bert was particularly fortunate to find that he excelled at the game during his Cardiff schooldays. He played centre three-quarter for the Welsh Schoolboy team at Cardiff Arms Park, and says without a hint of boasting that he feels he might even have won a full international cap if he hadn't been Italian. By the time he took out UK citizenship at the age of twenty-one it was, he asserts, too late.

Even as a youngster Bert's thoughts were turning to mechanical things, and on leaving school he took up a general engineering apprenticeship in Cardiff. 'With this completed I wanted to get into motor cars because I reckoned they were the coming thing, so I took a job with Fiat in Turin. I well remember the journey—I had to go by train and it took three days to get there! Bit different from now.'

He stayed in Italy for a year, but even in such a short space of time the young Italian-born, Welsh-bred engineer made his mark. 'Fortunately the company reckoned me, and I found myself riding mechanic to that great driver Felice Nazzaro in a Fiat for the Coppa Florio.' Augustus Bertelli was bitten by the twin bug of the motor industry and motor racing.

By now the First World War was looming and Bert returned to Britain in the hope of joining the Army. Ironically, considering his prowess as a sportsman, he was turned down on health grounds. 'I was supposed to have had a kidney complaint, but I didn't know anything about it,' he says, obviously still smarting at the insult to his fitness.

Fortune, however, smiled on him, in the form of a friend, Major C. W. Jordan, who was a consultant engineer. 'I was always designing

3

things, and I mentioned to Jordan that I had designed a radial engine for a flying machine. Jordan was so impressed he got in touch with Grahame-White's, who manufactured French aircraft under licence and ran a flying school with wooden biplanes at Hendon. They took me on to develop this engine of mine. Quite frankly I knew it was no good, but obviously I went, and stayed with them until the end of the war, doing development work.'

By now Bert was truly on the up. Although still only in his twenties he had behind him engineering experience which stretched from Cardiff to Turin, he was admired as a sportsman, and he was developing an aircraft engine of his own design. By this time too he had taken out UK citizenship, while still retaining his Italian name Augustus Cesare Bertelli. After all, you don't throw that away unless you have something even better and grander to replace it.

It was during his war years at Hendon that Bert met Vera, who was to be his bride in 1918. They married at Hendon and moved to Golders Green, while Major Jordan and that radial engine in which Bert had such little faith were once again to influence his life. 'Word had got around about my engine, and on the strength of its reputation Jordan, who had recommended me to Grahame-White's, was given a top job at a Birmingham firm called Alldays and Onions. They wanted to develop this engine and Jordan took me on. I still reckoned the engine was no good—I designed bad things as well as good—but we went to Birmingham nonetheless.

'Alldays and Onions were a general engineering firm who brought out a car at around the turn of the century and continued making these old crocks right through the war. They were an antiquated outfit, and during the war the Government asked old man Alldays to build a commercial vehicle, designed by another firm. He reckoned that, as his company manufactured such a vehicle, the Government should use his design but they wouldn't, so he told them where to go. He just wasn't interested. The Government retaliated by refusing to give him any other war contracts, and that was the beginning of the end. They went bust in 1925.'

Bert's time at Birmingham, however, was full of incident and provides a wealth of memories. 'Before I joined them they had bought out a firm called Enfield Autocar Company who also built cars, and the result of this takeover was the Enfield-Alldays car. During my time with them I designed a new Enfield-Alldays made up of bits and pieces that were worth picking out from their old models.

'I think it sold several hundred, although there was nothing special about it. In fact, it was quite makeshift really.' Makeshift or not—and Bert's racing exploits with the car make one think it was not—Augustus Bertelli, engineer, was now Augustus Bertelli, car designer. An important milestone had been reached.

These racing exploits with the 1½-litre Enfield-Alldays resulted in a number of awards, including a gold medallion won at Brooklands in 1921 with such a car and with Jordan named as entrant. For the Major was the boss and by this time Bert had become his right-hand man.

Another memory of those immediate post-war days is of a revolutionary car shown by Alldays at Olympia in 1919. 'It had a radial engine and had been designed by a chap called A. W. Reeves. This car caused a sensation due to its advanced chassis, and although it wasn't ready they got orders for hundreds. I had to try to help that chap Reeves with the car, but I had no faith in it. The firm asked my advice and I told them straight—that it would never be any good. It had poor performance and it was too unorthodox. Nothing ever did come of it.'

'Yes I remember that car—they called it the Bullet', said Vera. 'They had started work on it when Gus joined them. On the day we went up to see about the job we saw that car near the factory and Gus said: "That's it, I'm going to work on that car." He went straight over and just left me standing there.'

Radial-engined cars that couldn't be made to work, lack of Government contracts and the general state of the economy took its toll, however, and in 1925 the company collapsed. Bert, a brilliant engineer bristling with ideas, had left two years before when his department was closed down, and was out of a job.

Ever active in thought and deed, Bert wasn't down for long, although the next episode in his car-building career was destined for failure. 'Through racing at Brooklands I had become friendly with an extremely wealthy young man called Woolf Barnato, who had a large estate at Lingfield, Sussex. Being out of a job, I suggested to him that he finance me in building a Bertelli car. He jumped at the idea, and we set to building them at his estate.'

'We built three prototypes, based on the Enfield-Alldays chassis fitted with a single sleeve-valve engine on a principle developed by Burt McCollum of Glasgow. Our aim was to put them on the market, and Barny was in a bit of a hurry to do this. While they were being

5

built, however, he decided to turn them into racing cars, and we entered all three in a 200-mile race at Brooklands. But this was something of a disaster, as all three broke down due to engine trouble. After that Barny lost interest, and I was high and dry again.'

High and dry perhaps, but a link was soon to be forged between Bert and another young engineer which was to be directly responsible for saving the Aston Martin name. 'An *Autocar* journalist called Monty Tombs introduced me to a fellow called Renwick, who was a student engineer with Armstrong Siddeleys at Coventry. Renwick's parents had died leaving him a lot of money—about £50,000 I think it was—and he was looking for someone with the practical experience of designing cars. He was keen to have me join him and I very quickly agreed.' And so, in 1924, Bert and W. S. Renwick teamed up with a capital of £3,000, rented a factory in Birmingham's Tyseley district, and set about designing an engine with the aim of selling it to car manufacturers.

While Bert and Renwick were setting themselves up in business, a London-based car manufacturer was sliding towards obscurity. Aston Martin had its origins before the First World War, when Robert Bamford and Lionel Martin converted Singers for speed trial and hill climb use, and it was from one of these hill climbs at Aston Clinton, Buckinghamshire, that the name was conceived, but during the early 1920s Lionel Martin built cars carrying his own name and which were in the public eye through competing in racing both at home and abroad. In 1924 the company was taken over by the Charnwood family and run by the Hon. John Benson, who was later to become Lord Charnwood, but by the following year production had stopped and a receiver appointed. Bert remembers Martin, the Charnwoods and the sequence of events well.

'Martin was a great friend of mine—I met him regularly at Brooklands. He started off before the war with Bamford putting bits of Singer together at a place in South Kensington, but after the war they split up and Martin built his own cars at a factory in West Kensington, and called them Aston Martins. He built one or two cars which were fairly successful, such as 'Bunny', which was a very narrow racing two-seater. Actually, he was a bit of a pompous sort of bloke. He had quite a bit of money at one time, but Aston Martin used it all up. He practically lived at Brooklands.'

'Then, just about when we were setting up in Tyseley, Lord Charnwood took over Aston Martin from Lionel Martin for his son

6

John Benson. John was a university man—he had studied engineering at Oxford, I think it was, and he designed a new engine and tried to carry on the name. But he got through all the money and everything stopped. Renwick and I heard about it and we decided to have a look. When we got to the factory we were amazed—it was just a mews, little more than stables. Benson really had nothing but the goodwill of Aston Martin.'

Yet that goodwill was enough. 'Renwick decided to pay £4,000 for Aston Martin, and at my suggestion we kept John Benson on.' So, within two years of joining forces, Bert and Renwick were running a car company which had gained a reputation for building successful racers and high-quality production cars. Augustus Bertelli had really arrived.

The two moved out of Tyseley and took over a factory in Feltham, on the outskirts of London, and with them came a teenager who was also destined to carve a niche in the Aston Martin Hall of Fame—Claude Hill. 'We took Claude on soon after starting at Tyseley,' Bert reminisces. 'He was only a lad, and we put him in the drawing office. He was quite intelligent, and I took a great deal of interest in him—in fact, I almost treated him as if he was my son.' That 'son' was to have an influence on Aston Martin for more than two decades.

Bert and Renwick immediately started designing a new car, and with 'nothing but goodwill' as a foundation they had to start right at the beginning, except of course, for the engine. This they had been working on at Tyseley and which, although never sold to a manufacturer, had up to that time found itself in but one car, an Enfield-Alldays based prototype registered as an R and B but nicknamed the 'Buzzbox'. 'Within a year of starting at Feltham we had designed and produced a completely new Aston Martin. We'd done the lot ourselves—the 1½-litre engine, the gearbox, steering, back axle, everything.' It was available as a long-chassis saloon or open top, or a short-chassis sports version. Only a handful were made and sold, but the first hurdle had been cleared.

The end of the 1920s and the dawn of the Thirties saw the Aston Martin name carried on the 1½-litre first series which bore such famous names as International, Le Mans and Ulster, while the second series was in production during 1932 and 1933 and the third series during 1934 and 1935. That Tyseley-born, Bertelli and Renwick-designed engine gave nearly a decade of faithful service, but more than 50 years after its birth Bert is qualified in his praise of the unit. 'It was well designed and sturdy, but it was far too heavy to give really exceptional performance.'

Not that such a problem prevented Bert from enhancing the Aston Martin racing image during the late Twenties and early Thirties, or from gaining a host of awards and trophies which are still spread around his home. Brooklands, Ulster, Dublin's Phoenix Park and Le Mans were a quartet of racing circuits Bert can recollect today, while names with whom he shared driving include Penn-Hughes, George Eyston and Sammy Davis. 'We entered Le Mans regularly, missing out only when we couldn't afford to compete, and it was in these races that we gained the necessary experience to develop our cars.' Bert's living room bears testimony to his success by having in pride of place two magnificent trophies: the Rudge-Whitworth Cup, awarded after the 1932 Le Mans for fine performances in that year's, and the 1931, event; and a first-in-class award, also from the 1932 Le Mans.

Another notable achievement was fourth overall, and second in class, in the 1930 Brooklands Double Twelve, and it was that circuit which also gave Bert one of his greatest thrills. 'I've forgotten which year it was—it may well have been that 1930 race—but do you know my 1½-litre Aston was actually faster than a three-litre Bentley. Now that was really something.'

One of the aspects of the Aston Martins of the late Twenties and early Thirties which gained continued praise was their bodywork, both from the aesthetic and quality points of view. And for both a great debt of gratitude is owed, and by Bert readily given, to Enrico Bertelli. Enrico, or Harry as he was inevitably known, was Bert's brother, and he ran a coach-building business next door to the Aston Martin factory at Feltham. 'Harry used to build horse-drawn carriages down in Cardiff, and he occasionally made car bodies, so when we took over Aston Martin and moved to Feltham he joined us there.

'He was an artist. He used to make beautiful bodies far in advance of their time, and I have often been told that our 1½-litre cars were the most attractive of that era.' The bodies available with the 1½-litre series ranged from two to four doors and from two- and four-seater sports and coupés to four-seater saloons based on various chassis. It was an era of the genuine hand-built and individually-made car, with subtle bodywork differences appearing frequently—at least by today's standards—and even with just a chassis offered for sale to the public.

But behind the glamour of the racing scene and the artistry of Bert and Harry, all was not well. Reminiscences usually dwell on the good and on what the brain wants to remember, but Bert still recalls the hard times of running Aston Martin, the difficulties which the public never saw, and the heartaches which stretched everybody's loyalties to the limit. It is a side of this famous car company which has rarely been detailed, but which Bert candidly revealed in an almost defiant manner. It was as if he was glad to have got it off his chest after all these years. And surprisingly in view of the apparent success which Bert and Renwick quickly brought to Aston Martin, the problems were there almost from the beginning.

'Benson and Renwick continually quarrelled and argued—I think it was a case of Oxford University against Cambridge. Quite frankly it was my experience which kept them both on the straight and narrow, as neither of them had much themselves. I used to decide what we would do and what we wouldn't. I did the lot—controlling the factory, designing the cars, making them and selling them. I was head cook and bottle washer.' The team split up after about a year of being formed when Benson left the company, and it wasn't long before Renwick left too. Bert was well and truly on his own.

'During this time we employed about twenty people and roughly averaged one car a week' (Statistics prove that figure to be accurate, for a total of 425 first, second and third series 1½-litres were built between 1927 and 1935, an average of about 48 a year). 'They were very, very difficult to sell at their price, which was around £550 to £650. That was a hell of a lot at the time.'

The company was continually short of money, so much so that at times they couldn't even afford to pay the wages. Even the up-and-coming, highly respected Claude Hill left twice, in 1928 and again in 1934, when there wasn't enough money in the kitty to pay his wages, although each time he returned at the request of Bert. 'I sometimes went months without drawing anything simply because there wasn't enough money to develop what I proposed.' It was a begging-bowl existence for Bert, who spent as much time chasing finance to keep the little company together as he did using his considerable talent on improving the cars.

'During the bad times in the late Twenties and early Thirties I tried all I could to keep Aston Martin together, and various people

9

who I approached put in sums of money to ensure we kept going. Most of these people were customers who realised what a good car we built. I was glad at times to get anything so long as I could keep the name alive. It was a long and continual struggle. Among those who put money in were Sidney Whitehouse, a garage proprietor from Harrow, Percy Kidner, who had been a joint-chairman of Vauxhall, and in 1932, Lance Prideaux-Brune, one of our distributors. They had nothing to do with the day-to-day running of the company—they just wanted to see us continue.'

Another problem was that the company tried to do too much on its own. 'We designed everything, and that was as much our failing from the financial point of view as anything,' Bert admits. This policy changed with the introduction of the second series in 1932, and the use of outside parts enabled the International sports model to be reduced by more than £100, to £475. Yet still the financial problems continued.

Throughout this difficult period Vera was right at Bert's side. She accompanied him to race meetings and was always around when needed. 'We have always been as one,' she says. 'When we saw the workhouse looming in the distance I used to say to Gus: "You have done right before and you're doing right now. Everything's OK by me".'

The beginning of the end as far as the Aston Martin-Bertelli connection was concerned was 1932, when control of the company passed to Sir Arthur Sutherland. Sir Arthur's son Gordon was put in as joint managing director with Bert, who for years had been the loner, running Aston Martin against all the odds. The arrangement didn't work, with Bert finding it difficult to see eye-to-eye with the Sutherlands. In 1936, the year of the introduction of a new series of two-litre cars, Bert resigned. In his own words he had 'had enough.' The continual struggle, and the arrival of the Sutherland family, proved too much for him.

For a while the Bertellis continued their difficult times, and they were forced to rent out their lovely detached house in the Buckinghamshire village of Farnham Common and take a small flat in London, although such was Vera's pride that she told neighbours and friends that they were staying in London to watch the Coronation of King George VI! Bert took on what consultancy work he could get, mainly with Coventry-Climax, and he also worked with his brother Harry, who kept open his factory in Feltham even though Aston

10

Martin took over the building of their own bodies after Bert left them. During this period Bert, sensing that another war was inevitable, designed a two-wheel trailer which had a small Climax engine and was equipped with fire-fighting equipment. 'It was designed to be pulled by a car, and we built and sold quite a lot of them. They were widely used during the war.'

His talents, however, were soon recognised by the firm High Duty Alloys, who operated from Slough, just a few miles from Farnham Common. They took him on just before World War II, opened a factory for him to run, and called it Templewood Engineering Company after the lane where his house was situated. This was the break that Bert not only needed, but which he thoroughly deserved. It was a job which gave his creative qualities plenty of scope, a job on which he could concentrate without having to go cap-in-hand for money to develop his ideas, and a job which he acknowledges put him back on his feet.

One design which came from Bert's pencil during his spell with High Duty Alloys, and of which he is intensely proud, was for a grass-dehydrating machine. This ran on a conveyor-belt principle, and its advantage was that it dried grass without destroying any of its qualities and properties—a boon for the farmer in his feeding of livestock. And, not content with that, Bert also designed a complementary machine which cut and compressed the dried grass into small cubes, thus making the feeding of cattle even easier. But how did Bert come to design such a device? The answer lies in a move of home in 1940.

'It was then, not long after joining High Duty Alloys, that we moved to a farm in Wargrave, Berkshire, and there we had a herd of Jersey pedigrees and a herd of North Devon cattle. I wanted to keep Harry's workshop in Feltham busy and I turned to agriculture which, like motor cars just before the First World War, was the coming thing. So I designed this grass-drying machine. It was very successful.'

In 1955 Bert left High Duty Alloys and lived in semi-retirement on his farm until 1977 when, on doctor's advice, he and Vera moved to their present flat. Not long before that move he visited the Aston Martin works in Newport Pagnell, Bucks, and was seen to be continually diving into small nooks and crannies and curiously scrutinising all the equipment. He also had a ride in a modern Aston Martin, the V8 model, and afterwards enthused over the quality and

11

performance, saying: 'Do you know, I can even feel pride in that car.'

This, then, was Augustus Bertelli's own story, in which he reveals himself, probably more openly than ever before, as not only a brilliant engineer and designer, but a man of guts and determination. His success ranged from grass-drying equipment and fire-fighting trailers to some of the prettiest cars the world has ever seen, yet perhaps his greatest success of all lies not in what he produced from a drawing-board, but from what he produced in terms of other people's cash to keep the name of Aston Martin alive. His was a fight he refused to concede until, perhaps subconsciously, he knew was won, a fight which, today, means that Britain still has a company which, although small in size, is huge in reputation. No one had a right to expect Bertelli the engineer to spend much of his prime of life as Bertelli the saviour, but that is what he was.

The only nagging thought, perhaps the only regret, was what might have been if Bert had been born 50 years on, if he had been able to work in today's motor industry and been able to concentrate solely on engineering, a world he knew so well and a world where his talents would surely have been utilised to the full. It is a tribute to the man that, despite the diversions caused by the need to sell the cars and keep the factory alive, he was still able to give to the world the cars he did.

This story is best ended not by Bert himself, but by the wife who has stood by him through thick and thin. 'By sheer coincidence, Gus was very, very ill early in 1975, just when the newspapers were carrying the story that Aston Martin had collapsed. To be honest we thought he was going to die, and I remember thinking how ironical it was that this might happen at the same time as Aston Martin went.

'But Gus pulled through, and so did Aston Martin. Isn't that wonderful?'

One of the first Aston Martins to be built at Feltham by Bertelli and Renwick—the T-type 1½-litre saloon of 1927. Standing with the car is the Hon. John Benson, later Lord Charnwood, who ran the company before Bertelli and Renwick took over.

The photograph records a visit by Bertelli to Newport Pagnell in 1973. He is shown standing in the Service Department next to William Willson, Chairman of Company Developments Limited, who owned Aston Martin at the time, flanked by a Bertelli 1½-litre 2/4 seater Ulster and a current Aston Martin V8.

13

A twin cam, 16-valve, single-seater Grand Prix car built at West Kensington in 1925, a year after the Charnwoods had taken over Aston Martin from Lionel Martin. This example is a team car, originally built for Humphrey Cook to drive in the Junior Car Club 200 mile race. It crashed on the first lap. It disappeared for many years, being rediscovered in 1951. There followed some rebuilding, a partial one by Lord Charnwood, formerly the Hon. John Benson, and a complete one in 1957-8 by two more motoring enthusiasts. Its competition record since the rebuild has shown a marked improvement over its first outing, mostly in the hands of Derrick Edwards. From Lord Charnwood, the car passed into the hands of the late Dudley Coram, who was chairman of the Aston Martin Owners Club for 25 years, and then to Oscar Ruegg, a Swiss collector.

The same car in the hands of its present owner, seen at the Wiscombe Park Hill Climb in 1976.

A 1928 four-seater tourer 1½-litre T-type of the first series. This was one of the early cars fitted with the faithful Tysley Renwick and Bertelli designed engine.

A 1932 1½-litre of the second series. This is an early production version of the 2/4 seater Le Mans car.

The Company and the Aston Martin Owners Club held their first joint gathering at the Works in 1977. This picture shows some cars not usually to be found in the very modern Service Department. In the foreground is LM 21, a 1½-litre team car of 1935. Behind is LM7, an earlier team car which first appeared in 1931.

A 1931 team car, number LM6, driven in that year by Bertelli in the Brooklands Double Twelve, and the R.A.C. Tourist Trophy. It was also one of the three team cars that ran at Le Mans in that year's 24-hour race.

The third of the 1932 1½-litre second series team cars, number LM 10—the others were LM 8 and 9. Bertelli gained his first big international success with this car, winning the Rudge-Whitworth Cup at Le Mans, the team's only appearance in the 1932 season.

The last of the 1935 team Ulsters, LM 21, a picture taken at a sprint event in 1977.

A 2/4 seater Le Mans 1½-litre second series car built in 1933. From 1951 it was regularly raced for well over twenty years by the same owner, both at home and abroad.

Sprint events, circuit racing and hill climbs are all fair game to this 1½-litre Ulster. Its first season in 1935 saw the car in action in the 24-hour race at Le Mans and in the Mille Miglia in Italy.

2 Claude Hill

History can be most unfair. As a means of creating, or enhancing, a reputation it is second to none. But, by accident or design, it is totally discriminatory in whom it chooses to immortalise. Invariably it is the generals and admirals who are the subject of its favours, while the privates and the ratings are at best also-rans, at worst ignored. The Battles of the Somme and Waterloo may have been steered by the men at the top, but they were as much victories for those beneath.

Claude Hill wouldn't mind being referred to, in the historical sense, as a rating, even if his decisions and influence were of general proportions. He was a backroom boy who rarely shared the spotlight when it turned on Aston Martin, and a man who, today, is all too often by-passed by the historians. His name is hardly on a par with Bertelli or Sir David Brown, both of whom he served under, yet it is impossible to do justice to the story of Aston Martin without recounting the part he played.

There are, indeed, similarities between Claude and Bertelli which may be coincidence, but are more likely due to the strong influence Bert had on Claude during his early working days. Both tend to talk with their hands, and both have a deep conviction that what they designed was right. It is a conviction which, to a casual onlooker, may at times resemble conceit, but which is due entirely to a confidence in their abilities—and to the passing of time, which has shown that many of their engineering and design decisions were the correct ones. Bertelli and Claude worked like father and son, and when Bert left Aston Martin the protégé was fully equipped to deal with life at Feltham.

Claude, who now lives in contented retirement in his beloved

19

Warwickshire, was born in Birmingham in 1907, and spent his childhood within the environs of that sprawling city. The latter days of his studies concentrated on the unlikely combination of drawing, maths and English, with drawing being his particular talent. As early as 1923 he gave a clear indication of where his future lay by taking third prize in a Midland Counties competition for machine drawing. He was only 16, but the path ahead was already charted, and this soon led to a junior draughtsman-cum-office-boy job at the Spencer Sprinkler Company in the Birmingham suburb of Handsworth. This was followed by a move to Best and Lloyd, a motor accessory manufacturer, and it was while with this company that an advertisement caught his eye.

'I saw an ad for a junior draughtsman with an engineering firm called Renwick and Bertelli in Tyseley. There were 100 applicants for the job, but I got it.' So the young Hill was taken on at thirty shillings a week—'it was the time of the depression, and that wasn't a bad wage in those days for a lad of 17'—and the link between Claude and Bert was forged.

'Bertelli and Bill Renwick were designing a 1½-litre engine to sell to the trade, and when I joined Bertelli was drawing the cylinder head and Renwick the block. It was originally conceived as a long-stroke engine, but after testing they decided to lessen the stroke and increase the bore, which was the trend in those days. I did much of the draughting for this, and in fact drew the cylinder head for the revised engine. It was invaluable experience, and I took to it like a duck to water.'

Another early memory is of the one and only 'Renwick and Bertelli' car. 'It was nicknamed the 'Buzzbox' because of its peculiar exhaust note. It had the Tyseley-designed 1½-litre engine and front-wheel brakes, which was unusual, and I drew the front axle. The car could do 80 mph, and the first person to drive it was Renwick. It had cycle-type front wings, and on that first drive they fell off.'

Two years after joining Renwick and Bertelli, Claude found himself facing a move away from the area he knew so well, and down to London. He remembers vividly how the Aston Martin takeover came about. 'The *Autocar* journalist Montague Tombs, who knew Renwick and Bertelli, strolled into the drawing office at Tyseley and said that Aston Martin, which had been taken over from Lionel Martin by the Charnwood family not long before, was up for sale. They had been building side-valve engined cars, and our engine was a better, overhead-cam unit. Renwick and Bertelli went down to the factory at Kensington and decided to buy the company, although they kept Lord Charnwood's son on.

'They offered me a rise to £3.10s to go with them, and I went. I was very excited about it. They found a suitable place at Feltham, we moved in, and before long I was doing most of the drawings.'

Claude Hill was in his element. He was helping to design a car for a company which, although in its infancy, had already won a reputation which took other firms decades to earn, he was working for a father-figure who took a great deal of interest in him and who was ever-ready to guide and teach, and he had almost his whole working life ahead of him. For a youngster in the depressive years of the late Twenties, that all added up to a great deal.

Claude was a tremendous asset to Aston Martin. 'I had a sense of shape, movement, geometry and mathematics, and an intense desire to design and create. In fact I still feel that urge to create. I cannot stop. I often find myself thinking of such things as suspension systems or combustion chambers, or doodling with designs on anything— even paper serviettes.' His wife Lila nods in agreement. 'He never switched off, but I didn't mind. In fact they were good times.'

That desire to create and inability to switch off soon brought dividends to Aston Martin in the form of the International model, which was announced in 1928 at a cost of nearly £600. 'I started work on that car soon after moving to Feltham. I thought at the time it would be a fine car, but I didn't realise it would make history. It had a multitude of cross-members, a wide-track and a long wheelbase. But I do remember that it had a worm axle which frequently gave trouble. In fact we entered Le Mans the year the car was announced and that axle broke after seventeen hours.

'It was Bertelli's idea to compete at Le Mans, and we did it to prove the car under the most difficult racing conditions. He was always keen on racing.' Claude remembers Bert with obvious affection and regard. 'I used to see him every day. He was an instinctive engineer, but at the same time very practical, unlike Renwick, who had more theoretical knowledge.'

The late Twenties was a particularly stormy era at Aston Martin, even by the company's own tempestuous standards. 'The Charnwoods faded out in about 1927 and Renwick left about a year later. It was also in 1928 that Bertelli couldn't afford to pay my wages, so I very reluctantly left. I went to work on Morris engines at

22

Coventry. After about nine months Bertelli asked me to come back as chief draughtsman, and I went.' Claude hadn't needed much persuading.

Now at Feltham once again, Claude worked with Bertelli on improving the breed, using knowledge gained from racing plus their own instincts. The troublesome worm axle made way for a more reliable spiral bevel axle on the second series 1½-litres, which were built during 1932 and 1933, although the engine was basically similar. A total of 130 second series models were built—strangely, just one more than the replaced first series—and marketed under such names as New International and Le Mans, while a Standard four-door saloon or tourer was also available. Prices ranged from £475 to £625.

The dark clouds, however, still hung over the factory. 'It was always a struggle keeping going, because the cars were too expensive. We did have dealers around the country and we also sold a few abroad, such as in France. I also remember that an Indian Prince bought a 1½-litre. But it was never easy.

'After the Charnwoods faded out we had a succession of owners until Sir Arthur Sutherland took over in 1932. His son Gordon was crazy about cars, and he was made joint managing director with Bertelli.' The year of 1934 was memorable for the introduction of the third series 1½-litre range, called the Mark II—and the second departure of Claude from Aston Martin. Those dark clouds had descended enough to dry the kitty and force Claude to look elsewhere for a job. This he found in the chassis drawing office of the Vauxhall factory in Luton, but less than nine months later, at the 1934 Motor Show, Bertelli once again asked Claude to return, and once again Claude agreed.

The Mark II was a development of the second series Le Mans model and was available with various bodies, while the name Ulster—previously used for a more powerful engine option in 1930—was resurrected and given to a production version of the factory's racing cars. Claude is unstinting in his praise of the Mark II and the Ulster. 'The Mark IIs were certainly the best of the 1½-litres, and the Ulster was the prettiest car we ever made. Very nice.'

During the two-year production run of the third series, which extended to a total of 166 (including just 17 production Ulsters), Claude began work on an enlarged version of that faithful 1½-litre engine. 'We produced an experimental 1,750 cc engine by increasing the bore, and this gave us some valuable data from which we were able

23

to design a two-litre unit still based on the original engine Bertelli and Renwick had started while at Tyseley.' This two litre was first seen at Le Mans in 1936, but the racing accent which had prevailed for so long at Feltham was about to be replaced by a more determined commercial attitude. Gordon Sutherland's influence was being increasingly felt, and in 1936 Bertelli resigned, much to Claude's surprise. 'I had no idea that he was going to leave—it was a big loss to the company.'

Sutherland got Claude, who was made chief designer and engineer on Bertelli's resignation, to work on a detuned version of the two litre high-performance cars, and this resulted in the 15/98 (15 from the RAC horsepower rating, 98 from the bhp figure) of 1937. The Bertelli connection was well and truly severed with this model, as the bodies were now no longer built by brother Harry. It is an ironic reflection on enthusiasts and the motor industry that although, by Aston Martin standards, the 15/98 was a success, with approximately 150 being made, this model appears not to have the affection given to earlier—and later—cars.

Sutherland, who appears as a man never lacking in ideas, wanted a car of integral construction, and in 1938 Claude experimented by producing a car with a steel chassis, on to which was welded a steel superstructure. 'Sutherland was very keen to have rigidity, and this experimental car was certainly very stiff. But it was also very ugly, and was nicknamed Donald Duck for this reason.'

The boss, however, was keen enough to continue, and he commissioned Claude to design a completely new car based on the experiences with Donald Duck. 'I designed a four-door car which had a chassis and frame made of square and rectangular tubes, as I had decided that tubing was the best medium to use, bearing in mind the need for rigidity.' With this car Claude Hill had carried Aston Martin, in one giant leap, from what was arguably the past—albeit a very attractive one—to the present, for other features of this car included an automatic gearbox, fairly sophisticated steering geometry and, for the first time on an Aston Martin, independent front suspension.

Called the Atom by Sutherland—'because it had lots of performance in a small package' explains Claude—this newcomer was powered by the two litre version of the 1½-litre Tyseley engine, although by this time Claude had started designing his own, completely new, two litre pushrod engine. 'We finished the Atom early in 1939, and it was about then that I started work on my new engine. I carried on until the outbreak of war, during which the Atom was driven around by both Sutherland and myself.'

Aston Martin took on the uncharacteristic role of sub-contractor during the Second World War, with aircraft components being manufactured at the Feltham factory. 'I put my mind to the design of jigs and tools, and in fact I designed the tools that produced the Spitfire joy-stick.' But doubtless his mind was on that engine and the Atom, so as soon as time and the war permitted Claude, by now promoted to technical director, continued work on the new two litre unit, and one was soon fitted to the Atom.

'Immediately after the war I also set about re-designing the Atom's suspension front and rear to give a better ride and improve the road-holding, and I also made changes to improve its looks.' This re-designed car was an obvious basis for a new model, but a problem which wasn't exactly new to Aston Martin management reared its ugly head—a lack of cash. There wasn't enough money in the bank to develop a new car, so some was sought by way of an advertisement in *The Times*, and this resulted in a financial takeover by David Brown, although Sutherland remained as a director.

'I was in the drawing office working on the re-design of the front suspension when I first met David Brown—he was down at Feltham looking over the place before deciding to buy it.' With the new owner Aston Martin was in a position which, for them at least, was slightly unusual—there was enough cash in the bank to do some proper development work. But no one at that time realised how proper that work was going to prove to be.

'I got busy on developing the new car, and part of the work included a lone racing version for the 24-hour race at Spa in 1948, fitted with my new engine. We didn't have a lot of time for this, but with Jock Horsfall and Leslie Johnson driving we actually won. I went over to Belgium for the race and felt ill with excitement. It was the first 24-hour race Aston Martin had won outright, and it was to be another eleven years before it was to happen again. I couldn't believe it. After the race I got totally drunk.'

It is impossible for the layman to comprehend the feelings and emotion which accompany such a feat, but what makes this particular victory even more astonishing is that it was done with a hurriedly-completed car based on a design which was still in development and using an engine which was very much in its infancy. It speaks volumes for the skill and intuitive instincts that separate such designers as

Claude Hill from the pack, and it must surely be vindication for the importance placed on competitive driving by Bertelli and so enthusiastically pursued, when cash allowed, by Claude. It also says much for the new owner, David Brown, in that he realised the value—yet, at the same time, the dangers—of putting to the racing test a car which was to be, in production form, the launchpad for his newly-acquired company.

An elated Claude Hill returned across the Channel to Feltham and, with his confidence boosted, completed the work on the production version of the new car, and this made its public debut at the 1948 London Motor Show. Called initially the Two Litre Sports—but subsequently titled the DB1 on the appearance of its successor the DB2 in 1950—this car owed much to experience gained with the Atom, with its chassis and front suspension in particular being strikingly similar to those of the pre-war car. The specification included a David Brown gearbox, and it sold for nearly £2,400. An unsuccessful effort was made to cash in on the Spa success by offering a production version of the racing car, but the price of more than £3,000 put paid to that idea.

'The DB1 was entirely my car,' says Claude. 'I was, and still am, intensely proud of it, although there were several design features which I would not have now, such as the long wheelbase—nine feet—and the narrow track. But the idea was to make a luxurious, quiet sports car, and I think we succeeded.' About fifteen of these impressive-looking DB1s were produced, a number which was not great even in Aston Martin terms, but it did give everyone a little breathing space following the resumption of production after the war and the traumas of developing a new car and a new engine. All was set fair at Feltham, yet for Claude the end of an era was approaching.

Claude started work on a successor to the DB1, and among his ideas was a six-cylinder version of the four-cylinder, two litre pushrod engine. This was very much Claude's baby, but his hopes of this unit being fitted to the DB1's successor were thwarted by David Brown's decision, in 1948, to buy the car company Lagonda. This firm had on their books a six-cylinder engine of their own—indeed it was this as much as anything which influenced David Brown's decision to acquire Lagonda—and David Brown decreed that this, rather than Claude's, was to be the engine for the DB2.

'When David Brown bought Lagonda he decided to put their six-cylinder engine into a saloon car, and this was to be the DB2.' The

DB2, with a Claude Hill-designed chassis, made its appearance in 1950, although racing versions were seen at Spa and Le Mans a year earlier. 'The DB2 was reckoned to be the finest sports car made in Europe at the time. Its chassis gave stiffness, rigidity, comfort and cornering power—I regard it as the pinnacle of what I did.'

Regretfully though, Claude Hill was no longer an Aston Martin employee when the DB2 made its public debut in 1950, for a year earlier he had resigned following David Brown's decision to use the Lagonda six-cylinder engine rather than his. By this time, too, Gordon Sutherland was no longer with the company. 'After leaving I had about three months' rest, and then I had a telephone call from Freddie Dixon, who had interested Harry Ferguson in his idea for a four-wheel-drive chassis. Freddie asked me to see Harry, and after two to three visits I was offered a job at Ferguson Research as chief engineer. I was with the firm until my retirement in 1971.'

Another similarity between Bertelli and Claude is the way their careers with Aston Martin ended after a change of ownership, Bert quitting soon after the arrival of Gordon Sutherland and Claude after David Brown came on to the scene. Their leaving was probably all the more regretful because each still had a lot to offer, and with Claude in particular it is impossible to escape the feeling that he was never able to show his full potential due to constant interruptions—twice when he had to leave under Bertelli because they couldn't afford to pay his wages, and then with the outbreak of the war when the Atom and the new engine were being developed. Designing tools for Spitfire joysticks was a praiseworthy and totally worthwhile occupation, but it hardly enabled Claude, then in the prime of his life, to utilise extensively the design and engineering talents with which he had been endowed.

The war also meant the two litre engine on which Claude started work in 1939 had, particularly by motor industry standards, a ridiculously short production life, being fitted as it was to just the handful of DB1s built and to two of the early DB2 racing cars which competed at Spa and Le Mans in 1949. But Claude, who, as Sir David Brown reveals in the next chapter, left after a row over which six-cylinder engine would be used in the DB2, remembers mainly the good times. 'I was very happy during the early days at Tyseley, but equally enjoyable was the time I spent designing and producing the Atom, and the new two litre engine.' He has praise also for the evergreen 1½-litre Tyseley engine. 'It had a good breathing capability and therefore development potential, and it was also relatively smooth.'

Neither does he have any regrets at not being able to use his talents in designing cars for the Seventies and Eighties. 'When I see all the regulations for safety, emissions and so on I think "Thank God I worked on cars when I did." It was all so relatively simple.'

Again like Bertelli, Claude still feels enormous pride in the present car and the company which produces it. He visited the Newport Pagnell factory during an Aston Martin Owners Club open day in 1977, and he describes the latest V8 model as a 'very desirable motor car.' It is, he says, a little too complicated and heavy, 'although, of course, it has immense performance,' He admits to sadness when the company went into liquidation at the end of 1974, adding: 'It is a wonderful thing for the name to still be in existence.'

Claude's clarity of mind—an essential asset for a designer—is shown by what he himself describes as a 'photographic memory for dimensions.' 'I can remember the dimensions, for example, of the first engine I worked on, but I can't remember what happened last year.' And, to prove his point, Claude quotes the dimensions of the very first Tyseley-designed engine before the stroke was reduced and the bore increased. 'The bore was 63.5 mm and the stroke 117 mm!'

I wasn't about to argue.

A rare photograph of a very rare car. This is the Atom, designed by Claude Hill just before World War II and which was used throughout the war by Claude and Gordon Sutherland. It was the only one of its type ever built, although lessons learned from it influenced Aston Martin thinking for more than a decade.

A 1934 Mk 11 tourer built on the longer chassis. Claude Hill describes this series as 'certainly the best' of the 1½-litres.

A view showing the graceful lines of this model.

One of the 21 coupés built between 1934 and 1935 on the longer Mk 11 chassis. By now, the 1½litre was nearing the end of its reign.

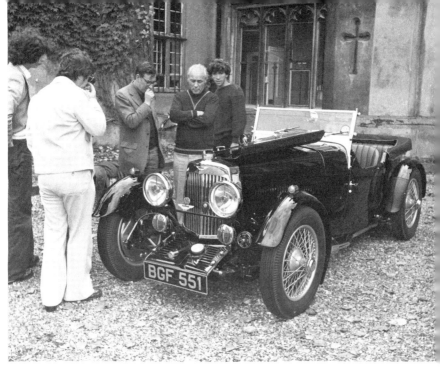

Another fine example of a 2/4 seater Mk 11, this one being built in 1934 on the shorter chassis. . . .

. . . and the engine unit which appears to be the object of the onlooker's scrutiny. The Mk 11 was introduced in 1934 and was the last model to be fitted with the Tyseley engine in 1½-litre form.

A 1935 Mk 11 saloon photographed with a suitable backcloth: a line-up of more modern Aston Martins at an Aston Martin Owners Club meeting at Wiscombe Park, Devon.

Two views of the Ulster—the front view of LM 19, a 1935 team car, and the rear view of LM 16, another team car built in the previous year. In Claude Hill's view, the Ulster was the prettiest car of the Bertelli era.

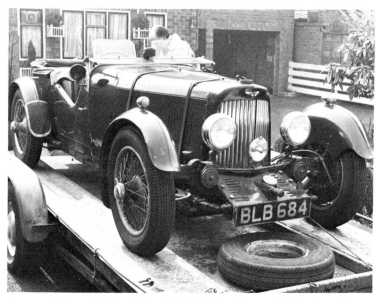

An unusual Ulster. This is a 1934 model, fitted with a 2/4 seater body in place of the more usual shapely two-seater version. This car is now the property of the Aston Martin Owners Club.

An early two-litre car, introduced in 1936. This particular example is known as a Speed Model and was destined to be the last of the cars inspired by Bertelli.

A 1937 15/98 2/4 seater seen at the last Aston Martin Owners Club concours d'elegance to be held at Fort Belvedere, Virginia Water, in 1975.

Another two-litre car of the 15/98 type in drophead-coupe form, this example being built in 1938. With the appearance of the 15/98 model, the firm took a conscious step away from their earlier highly sporting image. Not many of the type are to be seen today as they have never gained the enthusiast's affection given to earlier—and later—cars.

A 15/98 2/4 seater two-litre car of 1937. It is a regular competitor in motoring events and is driven to and from races both in this country and in Europe.

The 1922 Grand Prix single-seater in close company with a 1934 1½-litre Mk II.

One of the four last 1½-litre Ulster team cars built for the 1935 season. Their numbers were LM 18, 19, 20 and 21—this one being LM 19. The Ulster was one of Claude Hill's favourite cars '. . . the prettiest car we ever made'. For the second time the Rudge Cup fell to an Aston Martin. It was won by LM 20 and later that year, the cars took the team prize in the R.A.C. Tourist Trophy race.

One of the 2-litre Speed Models of 1936. This car was rebuilt in 1948 and again in 1949 when it was fitted with a new chassis. It ran in the 1949 24-hour race at Spa in Belgium where it came second in its class. It is seen here, still in winning form nearly thirty years later.

3 Sir David Brown

If Sir David Brown had visited a clairvoyant as a youngster it wouldn't have taken much expertise to forecast that, one day, he would own a car company. For if ever there was anyone destined to be such a line of business, it was him. Relaxing in his tastefully, and expensively, decorated London offices just a few days before the British tax laws had forced him to move to Monaco, seventy-three-year-old Sir David recalled how his ownership of Aston Martin came about. But before that he went back more than 100 years, to the very beginnings of what is now a vast industrial empire.

'My grandfather founded a pattern works in 1860 and this was carried on by my father. He in turn heard about gear-cutting machines which could be bought from Germany and this became the main part of the business, with the pattern-making side gradually fading out. In 1903 the business moved to Huddersfield—I am Yorkshire born and bred—and that is where we still operate from.' Sir David himself expanded to building tractors in partnership with Harry Ferguson in 1934 against the will of his father, who would have nothing to do with such a move, and as such he was heavily involved in the first Ferguson tractor. In 1951 the David Brown Corporation was formed with Sir David—still, at that time, unknighted—the chairman, while now the various activities come under the umbrella of David Brown Holdings, which embraces David Brown Gear Industries—probably the biggest manufacturers of industrial gears in the world—in addition to ship-building and offshore oil interests.

But while young David Brown was helping to build up this huge industrial concern he retained a deep affection for motor cars, and this love made itself manifest in the early Twenties when David, just a

39

young lad of seventeen, built himself a car by, as he succintly puts it, 'buying an engine and gearbox and welding it all together.' Showing a business acumen from the word go, David called this special a Davbro and even toured Scotland in it. During this period he also raced motor-cycles.

There was further contact with the motor industry during the 1920s when his family concern made a supercharger for Raymond Mays' Vauxhall Villiers racing car, and soon after came another accolade when Amherst Villiers commissioned them to build a Roots-type supercharger for the Le Mans Bentleys. 'This was a very difficult and precise job, and we had the gear-cutting machines to handle it,' recalls Sir David. The diversion into tractors was followed by the Second World War, and it was after this that Sir David saw an advertisement in *The Times* inviting offers for the purchase of a sports car company.

'This caught my eye and I replied, and you can imagine my surprise when I learned that it was Aston Martin. After all, that was a very famous name—I not unnaturally thought it would be a far less known company. So I came into contact with Gordon Sutherland and learned that he was renting a place at Feltham, in Middlesex. I went down there to have a look—this must have been at about the end of 1946—but quite honestly there wasn't much to see, except for the prototype they called the Atom.' Sir David's recollection of the limited facilities of Aston Martin bear a striking similarity to that of Augustus Bertelli when he visited the company's Kensington factory when it was run by the Charnwood family some twenty years previously.

'Anyway I decided to try the Atom and I took it up home, and put it through its paces over the Pennines. I liked it, particularly the superb roadholding, although it was a bit underpowered and not very good looking.' Sir David's love of motor cars and the attributes of the Atom won the day, and early in 1947 he became the owner of Aston Martin for the princely sum of £20,000.

The new owner quickly surveyed the scene and came to the conclusion that Aston Martin should market an open sports car rather than a four-door saloon, so Claude Hill and his staff set to strengthening the framework of the Atom, the result being what was later to be called the DB1. And it was around this time, hardly a few months after the acquisition of Aston Martin, that the wheels which

40

were to eventually lead to the purchase of another car company were set in motion.

'I was approached by Tony Scatchard, the Lagonda distributor in Bradford, who told me he was speaking on behalf of all distributors in the country. He said Lagonda was going into liquidation and urged me to buy the company. I told him 'not on your life—it is far too large a company for me.' As it happened I knew the Receiver, a Mr Greenwood, and a few days later he rang me up and invited me down to the factory, which was at Staines, Middlesex.

'I went down and found they had five prototype cars with a new six-cylinder engine, but I told Greenwood I had no intention of buying the company, as it was far too big a project for me. Greenwood said he had received three offers for the company, from Rootes, Jaguar and one other firm, who I've forgotten. Being an old friend he told me what the offers were, and the top one was for about £250,000. That proved it was too much for me. I must admit, though, that when I tried one of the prototypes I immediately thought that we could do with that new engine. You see, Claude Hill had already had the idea of developing a six-cylinder engine from his two-litre four-cylinder, but I'd told him we couldn't afford to put it into production.

'But back to Lagonda. Some time after I had told Greenwood I had no intention of buying the company Stafford Cripps came out with a gloomy economic forecast and I received another call from Greenwood. He said that, as a result of Cripps' statement, the three offers had been withdrawn, and I went down to Staines once again. Greenwood said there had been two further offers, much lower than the previous three, and he left them open on his desk deliberately and walked out of the room for a short while. I quickly discovered that the higher bid of the two was for £50,000, which was much more in my league. I offered £52,500, and Lagonda was mine. But we didn't get the factory for that, so I moved everything out of Staines and into Feltham.' So, within the space of about a year, David Brown had bought, for a grand total of £72,500, two of the most famous and prestigious car companies in the world.

The Lagonda engine which had impressed Sir David so much was designed by none other a figure than W. O. Bentley of car fame, who had joined Lagonda before the war but who retired when the company was merged with Aston Martin. 'When we bought Lagonda this six-cylinder engine was 2.3 litres, but we soon pushed it up to 2.6,' reveals Sir David. 'It was put into a prototype DB2, and I had a

41

frightful row with Claude Hill about it because he felt we should use the six-cylinder engine he was designing. But the Lagonda engine was an obvious choice—a number had been built and it was fairly well tested. It wasn't long after that Claude left.'

The success of the one-off Spa entry in 1948 had whetted Sir David's appetite for racing, although such was his enthusiasm that little whetting was needed. He decided to embark on a racing programme that carried the Aston Martin name on circuits in Europe and even the American continent throughout the Fifties and into the early Sixties, and which culminated in winning the World Sports Car Championship in 1959. Aston Martin is still, to this day, the only British car company to have won this prize.

'We started the programme with Spa and Le Mans in 1949. I was, and still am, a great believer in motor racing as being the only way to prove such cars as the Aston Martin although, having in mind the limited production, it is doubtful whether we were able to take advantage of the name we built up. After ten years of trying we won Le Mans in 1959, the year we also won the Worlds Sports Car Championship. Winning that race is one of life's great experiences, like flying solo for the first time.'

Racing was but one aspect of Aston Martin, albeit a glamorous and exciting one, and the main name of the game was to build production cars and sell them. 'Early on I devoted a tremendous amount of my time to Aston Martin, but I was gradually able to reduce this and delegate more.' One decision which Sir David personally made was to identify the various models with his initials, and this started with the DB2 (the DB1 was so named in retrospect) and went on to the DBS V8 of the early Seventies. Indeed there are a great many people today who refer to the present Aston Martin V8 as the 'DBS', including one world-famous ex-racing driver journalist who called it this throughout a road test report some five years after the initials had been dropped!

Models introduced during the 1950s included, chronologically, the DB 2/4, a four-seater which, like the replaced two-seater DB2, was available in closed or open form; the DB 2/4 Mk II and the DB Mk III, this being the last model whose chassis was based on the Claude Hill design starting with the Atom saloon before the war. All were powered by the Bentley-designed six-cylinder engine which grew from 2.6-litres to 2.9 during the production run of the DB2/4. 'We wanted to enlarge the engine, and one of our specialists, who used to work with Bentley himself, thought of the idea of staggering the cylinder bores, and by this method we managed to get it up to 2.9-litres,' recalls Sir David. Perhaps characteristically, Sir David reckons that the best of the cars of the 1950s was not a production model but one of the racers which kept Aston Martin's name in the public eye—the DB3, which made its public debut in 1951 and carried on competing until the 1953 Le Mans, when it made way for the DB3S.

In comparison with the previous production runs of Aston Martin, the early DB cars were built in enormous numbers, with more than 400 DB2 models coming out of the factory while both the DB2/4 and the DB Mk III each topped 500. Under David Brown's leadership Aston Martin was able to build on a sound commercial foundation, although even those DB production figures of the 1950s paled into insignificance with what was to come in the following decade.

Realising that the W. O. Bentley engine could not be expected to last for ever—in its 2.9-litre form it had probably reached its final stage of development—Sir David decided that work must begin on a replacement. 'I had a slight problem here in that we had a very good engine man but he wanted to retire. So we looked around and found a fellow called Tadek Marek working for Austin.' Tadek, a Pole, was taken on and discussions went on into many a night as to just what form the replacement engine should take. 'We had a V12 Lagonda engine which had been designed by Eberan von Eberhorst, a former Auto Union man who joined us early in the Fifties and who was responsible for the DB3 competition car. We had constant crankshaft failures with this engine, however, and there was a lot of heart-searching as to whether we should try to rectify the errors and make this the replacement. We also did quite a lot of talking around the possibility of a V8, but eventually we opted for a six-cylinder.'

Marek, as chief designer, started work on this new engine in 1955, and within two years it was put into the DBR2 racing car, the competition programme by now revolving around out-and-out racing cars rather than production-based models. The following year it was seen in a production car for the first time—the DB4, a strikingly-styled high-performance four-seater which brought Aston Martin right up to date in a way similar to that of Claude Hill's Atom twenty years before. The body was designed by Touring of Italy, and is regarded by a number of people as the most attractive Aston Martin

43

ever made, while Marek's engine, a 3.7-litre unit, featured twin overhead-camshafts and was all alloy.

'The DB4 was a completely new, and a very brave and expensive step,' muses Sir David. 'It had, for example, a strong platform chassis and wishbone front suspension, the geometry of which was the work of Harold Beach.' Mention of Harold, a man whose quiet influence from the early Fifties to the mid-Seventies was in the Claude Hill mould, shows how Sir David readily acknowledges the work of the backroom boys. 'I have a very high regard for him.'

With the DB4, Aston Martin leaped from the high-performance league to the ultra high-performance table, for while the DB production models before it ran out of steam at 120 mph and only one—the 2/4 Mark II—could beat half a minute in accelerating to 100 mph, the DB4 was capable of 140 mph and reaching 100 from rest in about 20 seconds. It was priced initially at nearly £4,000, some £500 more than the most expensive versions of the DB Mk III which, incidentally, was to be sold side by side with the new car for nine months.

Well over 1,000 DB4s were built in forms ranging from saloons to convertibles and including the Vantage and the GT, which came with standard or the stunningly-attractive Zagato bodies. It was during this model's run that entire production was moved from the Feltham factory where Bertelli and Renwick had begun in 1926 to the old Tickford bodybuilding factory in the Buckinghamshire town of Newport Pagnell, the present home of Aston Martin. It is also a reflection on the inflation—or lack of it—during this period that the final price of the standard DB4 before it was replaced was just £13 more than the cost nearly five years before!

The DB4 was replaced in 1963 by the similarly-styled (with the exception of faired-in headlamps) DB5, although beneath the bonnet Marek's engine had been enlarged to nearly four litres, in which form it was to continue until its eventual demise ten years later. Both the DB5 and its replacement, the DB6, also has production runs topping 1,000, the former achieving this milestone despite its comparative short life of just two years.

Opinions vary greatly—and inevitably—on which was the 'best' of the new breed of Aston Martins. Sir David puts his money on the DB5, while the DB6 gained many adherents due to the distinctive rear end, which incorporated a flat tail and a spoiler. What is indisputable, however, is that during this era the name of Aston Martin was heard like never before, due to a variety of reasons. Sir David's commercialism and ability to back up his, and others', ideas with hard cash was one; another was the racing and the victory in the World Sports Car Championship which came, by a stroke of good fortune, less than a year after the expensive-to-develop DB4 had been announced; yet another was in the incredible publicity, which rubs off even today, gained by the James Bond DB5 in the film *Goldfinger*; and, perhaps finally, there was the growing public awareness that Aston Martins were still built with meticulous care by craftsmen despite the increasing automation and demand for high volume which had overtaken almost every other car builder. The fact that Prince Charles bought a DB6 Volante (convertible) in its final Mark 2 form in 1970 didn't do any harm either, and indeed he is still seen regularly in the car, which is maintained by the present service department at Newport Pagnell.

Not that everything in the garden was lovely. 'There were times when it was comparatively easy to sell every car we made, and I believe we did at some stage reach a record output of twelve cars a week,' says Sir David—the present production rate, for example, is maintained at a steady six cars a week. 'But at other times it was difficult, and I recall that early in 1967 we cut the price by no less than £1,000 to reduce the stock.' This massive and probably unprecedented step cut the price of the DB6 at a stroke from just over £5,000 to a little more than £4,000 and was forced on the management by a stockpile of cars which, according to employees at the time, amounted to 200 cars. As one of the staff put it: 'There seemed to be cars everywhere—in cupboards, in fields around, in barns, and even in garages in the town.' It was a huge gamble by Sir David, and one which could have backfired due to a loss of public confidence in the company and a plunge in the value of second-hand Aston Martins. But it paid off, and within two years the DB6 had crept back to near its pre-price-cut level.

Aston Martin took what was, and still is, to some people a regrettable step away from building manoeuvrable, fun-to-drive, yet still sophisticated sporting cars with the advent of the DBS in 1967. This four-seater car, which had been seen in two-seat prototype form a year earlier, was to many a bulky and overweight model. Its width of six feet made it one of the widest cars on the market (six inches more than DB6 Mk 2, which it was destined to replace), while the kerb weight of 31¼ cwt was more than 2 cwt above of that of the DB6. It is worth noting that Bertelli's first International weighed in at a light-weight 18 cwt!

Sir David, who was knighted a year after the introduction of the DBS for exports gained by his various companies, admits to having reservations about the car. 'In my opinion it was too big and bulky, although it is a little-known fact that it was three inches wider than we had planned. This is because a mistake was made with the jigs, and when we discovered there was a three-inch difference from the drawings it was too late to change it, because we were under pressure from dealers to bring the car out. So it was built with a width of six feet, which means that the current Aston Martin V8, which is based on the DBS, is also three inches too wide!'

Features of the DBS included a body designed by William Towns, then an Aston Martin employee but who subsequently became a freelance and was responsible for the widely-acclaimed styling of the advanced four-door Aston Martin Lagonda which was unveiled in 1976; a platform chassis developed from that of the DB6, and a de Dion back axle, on a production Aston Martin for the first time. The engine was the Marek six-cylinder, but the DBS had been designed to take a brand-new engine on which work was actively proceeding at Newport Pagnell.

'With speeds increasing we decided to embark on the design of a new engine and we decided on a V8, a configuration which was under consideration when we were planning a replacement for the Bentley six-cylinder about ten years before. Another reason for designing a larger engine was that we knew Jaguar were working on a twelve-cylinder, and the fact that a few American sports cars were appearing with a V8 helped to influence which way we went. So Marek quickly got to work, and in fact we put one in a DB5 chassis, although it was too wide to fit properly.' Few knew of the V8-engined DB5, but the engine which, like Tadek's six-cylinder was all-alloy, became public knowledge when it was exhibited at the 1966 Racing Car Show and subsequently raced in two Lolas, without any success.

After a considerable development programme the 5.3-litre V8 engine became available in the DBS in 1969, the model not surprisingly being called the DBS V8, with the six-cylinder DBS continuing in production in either standard or more-powerful Vantage form until 1973. Like the DB4 before it, the DBSV8 took Aston Martin into yet another performance league, with acceleration to 60 and 100 mph in about 6 and 14 seconds respectively—and remember this car was considered too bulky and heavy by some!—

46

while the maximum was no less than 160 mph. 'A very fine car with fantastic performance,' is Sir David's assessment.

With the arrival on the scene of this V8-engined car, the factory at Newport Pagnell took on an unusually varied aspect, for in 1970 three different models were being built—the DB6, by now in Mark II form and available as a saloon or convertible, the six-cylinder DBS and the eight-cylinder DBSV8. It was a transitional period for the company, as the DB6 was nearing the end of its highly-respected life, the DBS was soldiering on admirably (800 were built between 1967 and 1972), and the V8 was just getting on stream. But all was not well with Sir David's business empire, and storm clouds were gather-ing which quickly led to yet another change of Aston Martin ownership.

'I was forced to sell because of various liquidity problems in the group as a whole. We had had to expand our tractor production from some 600 a week to 1,000-plus to fight the big boys, and this naturally involved a big and expensive expansion, and this was followed by a drop in world-wide tractor sales. In fact, I sold the tractor side at about the same time as selling Aston Martin.

'Naturally it was a wrench losing Aston Martin, but it was pretty obvious at the time that it would be difficult to produce a motor car of this kind and make a profit out of it.' Thus, early in 1972, Company Developments, a Midlands-based property company, bought Aston Martin, and another era in this illustrious firm's history came to an end. Sir David had owned Aston Martin for exactly 25 years, by far the longest time for it to have been in the same hands. When he took it over virtually the only assets were a prototype four-door saloon equipped with an untried engine, but during his reign it became a force to be reckoned with in racing and a leading specialist car manufacturer respected the world over.

Some may regard Sir David as a wealthy businessman who bought Aston Martin more for pleasure than any other reason, but the records prove otherwise. He may have had fun while it lasted, but is that a sin? The test is the opinion of those who worked under him, from management to the humblest clerk and from skilled panel beater to the youngest apprentice, and their feeling, gleaned from those who are still with the company, is that he was a good boss. Almost without exception they view him with a warm regard, and many look forward to his traditional visit to the company stand at the Motor Show—a tradition now regretfully broken due to his forced exile to Monaco. He retains a link with the company in that his wife still runs a DB6 estate car specially built for her when her husband owned the company, although Sir David's transport is now of a more stately, chauffeur-driven kind.

Despite his seventy-three years Sir David is still an extraordinarily active man, with a love of horses and tennis, and when talking to him one gets a feeling that he would do it all over again—given the chance.

The very first car sold under David Brown's ownership: THX 231 was the first DB1, having been built at Feltham in 1948.

A 1949 DB1, showing some pleasing lines of the first post-war Aston Martin. Of this model Claude Hill says 'it was entirely my car. I was, and still am, intensely proud of it.'

An early DB2, first introduced in 1950, using the six-cylinder engine which arrived with the acquisition of the Lagonda Company.

Another example of a DB2—this one being left-hand drive with Dutch registration plates. By now, export markets were becoming increasingly important as the Aston Martin fame spread through Europe in the wake of an extensive continental racing programme.

A 1952 drophead-coupe version of the DB2.

Believe it or not, this is a DB2. Serra, a Spanish coachwork company, put on the unique body in 1961 at the request of the British owner. The lines may be modern, but the size of the tyres give the age away.

During the production life of the DB2 the Company brought out its first purpose-built competition car called the DB3. This was largely the handiwork of Eberan von Eberhorst who was with the German Auto Union concern before World War II. Ten DB3 cars were built, this being number seven and the only one to have enclosed body work.

A late DB2/4. This model was a four-seat development of the DB2, although Harold Beach dismisses the rear seats as being no more than 'lavatory seats'.

One of the rare fixed-head coupé versions of the DB2/4 Mark II, built in 1955.

A very special DB2/4 Mark II, built in 1956, with coachwork by Touring of Milan, an early contact with the firm that was to become very closely associated with Aston Martin with the arrival of the DB4. Records show that three DB2/4 Mark II chassis were supplied to Touring. This particular example was offered as a prize in a newspaper competition.

A 1958 DB Mk III which has only recently come into the hands of its second owner, shown in its original production form which featured dual-tone paintwork. The coachwork is by Tickford, whose premises at Newport Pagnell are now the home of Aston Martin. David Brown acquired this small coachbuilding concern in 1956. It had made quite a name for itself with its development of a hood which was designed to be raised and lowered by mechanical means.

The same car, looking even better in its new paint.

One of the most attractive cars ever to have come from Aston Martin. This is one of what are now known as the short wheelbase Volantes, a retrospective naming to differentiate between it and the later DB6 convertible, built on a longer chassis. It has the DB5 wheelbase and instrument layout but uses the quarter bumpers which are to be found on the DB6. The trim style is also the same as the DB6. The shape of the rear wing is unique to this model and is one of the car's most attractive features. Its production life was one year between 1965 and 1966 and only thirty-seven were made.

An unusual type of coachwork to be found on a Grand Touring car. Twelve of these DB5 'Estate' cars were built, though none of them was done at the works. They were all originally saloons and were converted, mainly by Harold Radford.

The successor to the DB5, introduced in 1965 and called the DB6. It was longer than the DB5 and as a result, carried its occupants in greater comfort. Technically very similar to its predecessor, but power steering was available for the first time. Note the swept-up boot lid—a feature which still causes argument between the 'fors' and 'against'.

The first of the two prototype DBS two-seaters. This was the last model to be built in collaboration with Touring of Milan and it appeared in 1966. This car has right-hand drive and is strictly a two-seater car, built on a modified DB6 chassis with a de Dion axle at the rear, the first production use of a type which was fitted in the later DBS.

As with the earlier models a convertible DB6 Mk 2 was also available. This was to be the last convertible Aston Martin made using the Marek six-cylinder engine. Only thirty-eight were built and their rarity has made them much sought after.

An almost unique situation—six of only thirty-eight DB6 Mk 2 convertibles ever made, all to be found in the Company's Service Department at Newport Pagnell at the same time.

This is believed to be the only estate version of the DBS—again a specialist conversion, this time by FLM Panelcraft in 1971. It was commissioned by the first owner of the car and was originally fitted with a full length luggage rack, adapted to carry fishing rods.

Not the easiest of rear ends to adapt to this form but a very creditable result nevertheless.

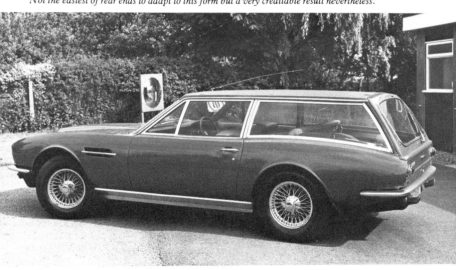

The second of the two prototype DBS cars made on the modified DB6 chassis. This was the last example of Touring coachwork on an Aston Martin.

There are not many opportunities to be had for building specialist bodywork on British cars since only a few, which include Aston Martin, have a separate chassis. Here is an example of an approach by Ogle Design seen on one of the two rolling chassis that were supplied to them for the purpose, in the early seventies. It was originally called the Sotheby Special but here bears the name of Embassy, another well-known brand name from the same cigarette manufacturer.

Its rear view is probably the most striking, being finished with a stainless steel panel, having a brushed effect, and using sequential indicator lamps (the upper row) and a series of brake lamps (lower row) the operation of which depended upon the severity of the brake force being applied.

A unique instrument layout of a DB5. This single example is the work of Ogle Design and featues extensive use of leather in place of the more usual vynide material.

A competition DB3 with three twin-choke Weber carburettors. . . .

. . . and a DB3S, the main difference from the early DB3 being the size of the engine, with the main unit being increased from 2.6 litres to 2.9 litres.

The V8 engine, as it was first used in the DBSV8 in 1969.

A redesign of the air box layout followed soon after. This gave better air supply to the carburettors and considerably tidied up the general appearance of the engine compartment.

The scene at Newport Pagnell towards the end of 1966—many new cars but not so many buyers. The situation was changed dramatically in February 1967 with a £1,000 decrease in the retail price.

The main venue for the concours events held by the Aston Martin Owners Club was Fort Belvedere, near Virginia Water, formerly the home of the Duke of Windsor. The main picture shows a line up of non-competing cars, those in the foreground being DB6 models.

A DB2 attacks Bunny's Leap at Wiscombe Park.

The classic lines of a DB4 convertible.

4 Harold Beach

Harold Beach is a man noted for the meticulous care he takes with his design work, the thoroughness with which he deals with every detail, his accuracy and his sharp engineering brain. In other words, a man made for Aston Martin, as if the company had been born to take advantage of what he had been endowed with. It is indeed fortunate for both—but particularly for the company—that they came together.

London-born Harold, who retired at the beginning of 1978 at the age of sixty-five, started his working life as an apprentice in the engineering department of the now-defunct, but still famous, coachbuilding firm of Barker's. 'I had always wanted to be a draughtsman without giving any other job a second thought,' says Harold. The year was 1928, and young Harold started at thirty shillings a week—coincidentally, the identical wage with which Claude Hill had started his engineering life with Bertelli four years before.

Barker's, famous for their craftsman-built Rolls-Royce bodies, had an engineering department principally staffed by men from the old Napier aero-engine works at Acton. 'There were some fantastic people there, and much of the equipment also came from Napier's. I couldn't have had a much better start.' After spending his early days at the Kensington factory Harold moved to the drawing office, and found himself working under 'an absolute tyrant.'

'I remember him calling me over one day and telling me that if my printing work did not improve by the weekend I would be fired. When I got home I told my father, and he said that if I got the sack he would strap me. I worked day and night on that printing, and I saved my job.' If that tyrant could see Harold's drawings and design work now, he would know the message had well and truly sunk in. Even a hand-written memo from him is a work of art.

A member of the aristocracy was soon to enable Harold to work on cars which even now would set any engineer's heart racing, let alone that of a youngster in the depressive late Twenties and early Thirties. 'Viscount Curzon, later Lord Howe, was a director of Barker's, and we became involved in his racing activities. So I found myself working on such cars as Bugatti, Alfa Romeo, Delage and Mercedes, and I was fired with enthusiasm for racing. The first 1½-litre, eight-cylinder, supercharged Grand Prix Delage to arrive in this country came into our workshops. Can you imagine how I felt—I regarded it with awe. That straight-eight engine was like a watch. It was a fantastic machine, the pinnacle of automotive racing design of its period. And there was me, a draughtsman not yet twenty, being able to do some design work on it. What a magnificent grounding!'

That grounding, however, was to come to an abrupt end in 1933. 'This was still the time of the Depression, and Barker's were not very progressive from the design point of view with their Rolls work. Firms like Park Ward were outstripping them all along the line except for quality. Why, they even persisted in carving their bodies out of ash. I saw the writing on the wall and I left, realising they would soon go out of business, which they did. The last thing I wanted was being out of a job—they were hard to come by at that time.'

With design work on the romantic motoring names of the era behind him, Harold went to the opposite end of the vehicular rainbow. 'I got a job as a draughtsman with William Beardmore, who built commercial vehicles at a factory at Earlsfield, near Wimbledon. I stayed there for three years designing these commercial vehicles, which was something I had never done before. Quite frankly, I regarded it very much as a stop gap.'

Meanwhile another ex-Barker's employee was setting himself up in business. 'He was James Ridlington, who used to be manager of the firm's engineering department. He bought a lot of the department's equipment and made components for Rolls and other firms. I joined him in 1936 and stayed until the war.' It was during this spell with Ridlington that Harold became even more deeply involved with racing—and with a car that was, and still is, unique. 'A wealthy cotton-mill owner called E. R. Hall persuaded Rolls-Royce to provide him with a 3½-litre, six-cylinder production Bentley for the TT race in Ireland, and it was the first, and still only, time that Rolls backed a private entrant. I designed the body of this car, and had it made out of alloy, which was something I had been interested in for some while as a means of saving weight. That car competed in the TT for three successive years leading up to the war.'

The war heralded yet another change of job for Harold. 'A brilliant Hungarian engineer called Straussler had formed two companies, one of which produced military vehicles, and indeed it was he who invented the floating tank which was used on D-Day. I joined him at his Park Royal factory as a designer and spent the war working on airfield components—testing equipment and that sort of thing. I stayed on with him after the war for several years while we tried to involve ourselves with other activities which never came to much.' Then, in 1950, Harold spotted an advertisement in the *Daily Telegraph* which was to set the course of his career for the remainder of his working life. After four jobs in not much over twenty years, he was, unknowingly, about to settle down!

'The ad was for a design draughtsman for the David Brown Tractors (Engineering) Automobile Division at Feltham—in other words Aston Martin. I knew David Brown had acquired Aston Martin and Lagonda and I thought: "This is the job for me—it must be." I applied and got an interview, and little did I realise that this was to result in more than half my working life being with Aston Martin. Anyway I was seen by the chief draughtsman called Frank Ayto, who was an ex-Bentley man and who came from Lagonda when David Brown took the company over.

'I thought the interview went quite successfully but then it came to money and I said I wanted £11 a week. Frank said that was 10 shillings more than he was empowered to authorise and that he would have to get in touch with James Stirling, the general manager. I remember him vividly as a Scot with a brilliant command of the English language. He came down to see me and gave me such a grilling that I thought I had no chance of the job. I went home and told my wife to forget it, because they were obviously after a genius. Imagine my amazement when, a few days later, I got a letter asking me to start at Feltham. And I did, in September, 1950.'

Not long after, however, Harold's enthusiasm and undisguised excitement at working for such a famous company received something of a jolt. 'I quickly got to know a fairly senior member of the staff and he asked me why I had joined, adding: "I'll give this company to Christmas." I wondered what I had done and whether I had made the

69

right move after all, but I soon realised that his pessimism was unfounded. I also met David Brown and was most impressed by his fantastic enthusiasm. If anyone had misgivings about a tractor manufacturer taking over a company building exotic cars, all they had to do was meet him.'

Although he wouldn't admit it, Harold must have impressed a lot of people. He had under his belt experience on working with such cars as Bugatti, Delage, Alfa Romeo, Mercedes and even a racing Rolls-Bentley, had put his mind to commercial vehicles and airfield equipment, and had been subjected to a training in his formative years which was to help carry Aston Martin through some difficult, as well as successful, years. Stirling had expected a genius, and there are some who would say he got one.

'I started work on what was planned to be the successor to the DB2, production of which had started earlier in the year I joined the company. Under Jock Stirling this work was to drag on for a couple of years, and meanwhile a lot of work was also going on with Lagondas at the same time. During this time Eberan von Eberhorst was made chief engineer, and this was a sensational event. There was this world-famous racing car designer—he was with Auto Union before the war—descending on little Feltham.' But Harold's delight was not to last. 'Eberhorst saw all our work on the DB2 successor and scrapped the lot. He had different ideas.'

Not the least of those different ideas was on the front suspension. 'I thought that the Claude Hill-designed suspension of the DB2 needed revising, from trailing links to wish-bone, for the new car, but Eberhorst didn't. He was something of an advocate for trailing links, and this is what was fitted to the racing DB3, which he designed.' But, not for the last time, one of Harold's ideas was to be incorporated later.

Harold accepts Eberhorst's decision to scrap their work philosophically. 'I knew which way I was supposed to be going with the DB2 replacement, but I naturally accepted the decision. But it was a lot of work wasted.' Perhaps, though, his real feelings can be detected with his assessment of what was to become, in 1953, the DB2's successor, called the DB2/4 on the strength of having four seats instead of two. 'This car was really only a development of the DB2. There was a great demand for four seats and, in my opinion, it was a marketing error to have restricted the DB2 to just two seats. But I used to call the back two seats of the new car lavatory seats. . .'

Harold was soon to start work on a replacement for the DB2/4, and this was called Project 114 from its number in the company's project register. His beloved wishbone suspension was planned for the front, a de Dion axle for the rear, while a perimeter-type frame was to replace the tubular structure used at the time and based on Claude Hill's ideas with the Atom saloon. 'Quite frankly the tubular structure was rather too flexible, and this to my mind was an important disadvantage.' This replacement was to be a completely new car, and Harold's influence was evident everywhere. Once again, however, his plans were to be thwarted.

'We produced a prototype and this was running around during 1954 and 1955, fitted with the 2.9-litre engine which was fitted to later DB2/4 models built. It is interesting to note that even this early the car was designated the DB4. My reaction on driving it was that the roadholding and handling were fantastic. It was driven many thousands of test miles, and while we were testing the chassis, suspension and other parts it had simply a test body, but then it was fitted with a proper four-seater body for David Brown and his wife to use as a personal car.'

A new appointment within Aston Martin, however, was to subsequently alter Harold's plans and, although the change was something of a shock, he readily admits that the decision was the right one. 'John Wyer, who was appointed competitions manager in 1950— and who was so often in conflict with Eberhorst in that he wanted to race the cars while Eberhorst always wanted to hold back for improvements—was made general manager in 1956, and I was made chief engineer. He had this idea that we should go to Touring of Milan for them to style a body on my perimeter frame, and you can imagine my shock when they turned round and said they would not build on my design, but instead wanted a platform frame.

'I was sent to Milan to liaise with them over the design of a platform frame that would fit in with the type of body structure they proposed, although the front and rear suspension of Project 114 was retained, with more up-to-date ideas. I was going to and fro between England and Italy as I had work with Touring quite a bit. They were a fantastic crowd. When you think of it, it was a major exercise to turn my proposed perimeter frame, which regarded the chassis as separate from the body, into Touring's idea of a platform frame, which viewed

71

the chassis and body almost as one and far more integrated. I really accepted this idea of regarding them as one rather than as separate entities because of the tremendous weight-saving and improved stiffness.'

This 'Superleggera' (super-light) principle, which in essence involves a strong platform chassis and a steel frame-work, onto which are fixed the body panels, is lighter because some components—for example the wheel arches—are part of the chassis and not added afterwards, while at the same time stronger because this integrated design adds stiffness. 'It is worth noting that Aston Martin has used the principle ever since and continues to do so,' Harold points out.

It is at this juncture that another respected Aston Martin name gets into the act—Tadek Marek, the Pole who joined the company from Austin in 1954 as chief designer. 'His first job was to do some re-design work on the 2.9-litre engine—in fact I also did some modifications to that engine and produced a more powerful triple-carburettor version—and after that he started on a completely new engine which was destined to be fitted to the DB4. He and I worked very closely together, and I found him to be a clever chap.'

While work was progressing on what was to be the all-new DB4, a Mark II version of the DB2/4 was introduced—the difference between that and the first DB2/4 being dismissed by Harold as 'insignificant'—and that was followed by the DB Mk III, which featured Marek's re-designed 2.9-litre engine and a handful of which were fitted with Harold's triple-carb unit. Harold describes the Mark III as a 2/4 Mk II with a different grille and instrument panel.' The latter change, he says, was because the old fascia was 'a bit ancient'.

The summer of 1957 saw a milestone reached in the history of Aston Martin, for the first DB4 prototype took to the road in July of that year. 'It had Marek's engine, Touring's body and my chassis and suspension,' says Harold proudly. 'I was immensely thrilled with it, especially when you remember that it was the first car completely designed by the company under David Brown. I remember that we worked night and day to complete the prototype by a certain weekend, and I drove it home to Pinner for the weekend in case John Wyer, who was away somewhere or other with David Brown, rang to ask about it. He used to ring me nearly every night—time meant nothing to him.

'Anyway on his return Wyer did ring and I told him I had driven it home—that was as far as it had ever been driven. There was our first all-new car and lo and behold, I told him it was in my drive. He suggested that I pick him up in the car the next day from his place in Fulmer, Bucks, and then we drive on to David Brown's farm, which wasn't all that far away. We arrived at the farm and David Brown got behind the wheel and really motored it at terrific speeds. It had never been more than 30 mph, and there we were tearing around the Chiltern hills with Wyer in the front passenger seat and me in the back. David Brown is a magnificent driver, and it was one of the most exciting things of my life.

'That car went really well, and David Brown was thrilled. It was fantastic, in a completely different world from the handling and roadholding points of view in particular. When David Brown had finished he said to me: "This is a very promising motor car," and I said "Thank you, Mr David." When it was unveiled the following year the Press reaction was excellent, and I recall Autosport describing it as Aston Marvel.'

By the time the car was in production, however, one of Harold's plans—the incorporation of a de Dion rear axle—had been shelved, because it caused problems when mated to the mandatory David Brown-built gearbox. Ironically the DBS of ten years later was to incorporate a de Dion rear end, thus making it the first production Aston Martin to be so fitted. Not for the first time had Harold Beach thought of an engineering idea which was to be subsequently adopted. 'The problem was that, when using a de Dion axle the transmission was too noisy, and the David Brown works could not make it sufficiently quiet, so we decided to adopt a different rear axle.'

One accusation which could never be levelled against Aston Martin under David Brown's ownership was that they stood still. He had the money and within the management had the expertise to progress continually, and even as the widely-acclaimed DB4 was in its five-year production run discussions started not only on an immediate successor (the DB5 was introduced in 1963) but on what would ultimately replace Marek's engine. 'We started talking of a replacement engine as early as 1962, only four years after it had been introduced in the DB4, simply because of the long period needed to design a new unit." Harold explains. 'There was a feeling that the days of the large six-cylinder were numbered. We talked around the idea of a V12, but it was David Brown's decision to make it a V8, and we unanimously supported this, for there was really no doubt that a V8 it had to be.'

The year of 1963 not only saw the debut of the DB5, fitted with an enlarged four-litre version of Marek's engine, but considerable upheaval within the company which could have had far more serious repercussions than in fact proved the case. 'For a start John Wyer suddenly decided to leave to go to Ford, and this left a great vacuum. We were then descended on by people from the company's tractor division, and their first move was to transfer us from the factory at Feltham, which housed the service, design and racing facilities, to our other factory at Newport Pagnell where at that time the DB4s and then the 5s were being built.' That Buckinghamshire factory, which still houses the Aston Martin works, came within the DB organisation in 1956, when the company bought the coachbuilding firm of Salmon's, who built bodies under the name of Tickford.

'At Feltham we had a well-established design team who were suddenly faced with the prospect of moving to Newport Pagnell. The M1 wasn't open that far then, and the journey was more like a day trip out in the country. We all regarded the town as being out in the wilds, and it's not surprising that there were serious misgivings. In addition there was no offer of disturbance allowance, help with housing or anything like that, and most of my twenty staff queried whether they should move or not. But David Brown learned that at least three-quarters of the design team were prepared to move—I have no idea where he got that figure from.

'Anyway the decision was made to move out of Feltham and transfer everything to Newport Pagnell, and David Brown soon learned how wrong his figures were when only two of the design staff—Marek and myself—agreed to move. So we came up with no staff whatsoever, and were faced with the prospect of recruiting new people with no experience. Just think how much experience we lost overnight because of that decision.

'At the time I was working on the chassis of what was to be the DBS, and one of the new people I took on was a chap called William Towns as a trim designer, as I had always believed that there was a need for someone to pay a lot of attention to this sort of detail from the production point of view. Towns came from Rover and it was soon obvious that he had a flair for styling. David Brown saw one of his drawings and suggested to me that he should do some of the styling for the car we were working on. Towns produced some proposals, and that is how the DBS body was created.' Since then Towns has hardly looked back and has won wide acclaim as a stylist of some note, his most famous work probably being the present Aston Martin Lagonda on which he worked as a freelance, having left the company to exploit his talent in a variety of directions.

Harold says that both he and Marek considered that the DBS was too wide and unwieldy, and even today he considers that the V8 model, which is its direct descendant, is too big. 'Having said that though, I think the styling is excellent, and I agree with those who now regard it as a classic.' The DBS was introduced in 1967, with Harold being responsible for the chassis and suspension, and it is worth recording that one of the features was a de Dion rear axle, a feature which was at last used a decade after it had first been proposed for production by Harold. 'It took ten years for that idea to become a reality,' he says.

That DBS was introduced with Marek's six-cylinder engine, but from its conception it had been designed to take his V8 unit on which talks had started way back in 1962. 'We had been running a DB5 chassis fitted with a V8 for some time, and that engine really was fantastic, although I must admit that we had all sorts of troubles with it after Marek left in the late 1960s before it was finally announced late in 1969 in the DBS body. As with the progress from the Mark III to the DB4, so the change from the six-cylinder engine to the V8 moved us half a dozen rungs up the ladder.' One of the features of this engine was the fuel-injection which was to give trouble within a few years by making it difficult to modify the engine for the tough U.S. emission regulations. 'We decided to revert to carburettors and this was a wise move, as we realised early on that the belief that injection made it easier to comply with the regulations was simply not correct. I spent a lot of time with Bosch in Stuttgart, who made the injection equipment, trying to sort out the problems, but they couldn't be overcome.' So, in 1973, a revised V8 engine incorporating four twin-choke Weber carburettors was unveiled, and in little over a year those emission requirements were met.

In 1972 Sir David Brown, who had owned Aston Martin since Harold joined them some 22 years previously, sold out to a Midlands-based property company called Company Developments, and the new owners brought in a firm of engineering consultants. 'They interviewed me and decided to keep me on,' says Harold blandly. 'During 1972 I worked very closely with them and got to know them well. In 1973 the chairman, Mr William Willson, made me director of engineering and the consultants departed.'

By Sir David's standards the Company Developments ownership was very short indeed, although the shortness of the tenure would have made Bertelli feel very much at home! On the last day of 1974 the production side of Aston Martin was closed down although service and parts kept going under a Receiver, and for months it seemed that Aston Martin Lagonda would no longer be a car builder. But Bert and those who followed him did not work in vain, for in June of 1975, with newspapers around the world following their every move, Peter Sprague and George Minden signed on the dotted line and saved what was essentially a British heritage.

Harold continued working with the new owners, although no longer as a director, and early in 1978 he retired, in a manner as quiet as everything he did. To say he will be missed is a classic British understatement. He is no longer there to turn to for historical information, technical details, or help with the hundred and one problems facing an active company like Aston Martin. No longer can a question be answered with the simple reply: 'Ask Harold, he'll know.' He devoted more than half his working life to the company, served under three ownerships, and had enormous influence on a range of cars now respected the world over. In some respects he was arguably ahead of his time, and undeniably ahead of some of those around him, yet at the same time his inbuilt modesty allowed him, as with Touring's ideas on the DB4 construction, to acknowledge when his thinking was wrong.

It can't be coincidence that two of the cars which bear his stamp—the DB4 and the current V8—are now regarded by many as classics worthy of a place in any motor museum. On introduction they were both considered to have a superb performance which was matched by the handling and roadholding, and it is to Harold's—and indeed, Marek's—credit that they were jointly able to merge their talents into producing such thoroughbreds. Harold is in the Claude Hill mould of being a quiet and talented innovator who made his mark simply by doing an outstanding job. There are others whose names are more associated with the products from Feltham and Newport Pagnell than these two, yet there are few who had more influence.

As Harold said of his 1950 interview: 'Obviously Jock Stirling was after a genius.' I wonder if he considered he got one.

Harold Beach standing beside a rolling chassis, before it left the Feltham Works on its way to Carrozzeria Touring in Milan where it was destined to become the first DB4. The Chassis design for this model was very largely Harold Beach's work.

It was to be eight years after the introduction of the V8, before this totally new convertible made it's appearance in June 1978.
Like many of the preceding convertible cars it is known as the Volante, and it is the last model to bear evidence of the craftmanship of Harold Beach who was primarily responsible for it's design.

'A very promising motor car' was how David Brown described the DB4 after driving it for the first time in 1957. This model featured a new six-cylinder engine, Harold Beach-designed chassis and suspension, and a Touring body. The photograph is of a 1961 Series Two version.

A convertible from the fifth, final series of the DB4.

A year after the introduction of the DB4, the firm brought out what was arguably its most exciting car, the DB4GT, and this was how the car in the photograph started its life. Its present form is the result of a total rebuild at the Newport Pagnell works in 1967-8, which entailed the complete removal of the body from the frame. The front panelling is DB5, the rear, a modified DB6 complete with that model's characteristic swept-up tail. The doors were specially made, and used Italian flush-fitting door handles. The interior trim was DB6 in style and the stereo tape equipment was specially imported from the United States.

Special plates were made for the engine compartment and the door sill to testify to its origins and a one-off instruction book was printed also.

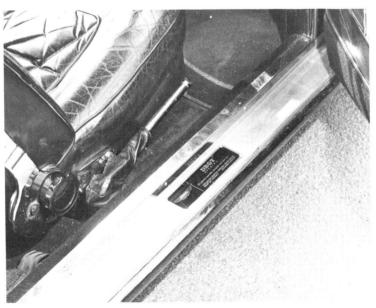

A more familiar looking DB4GT. This is a 1960 car and one of the small number of lightweight GTs and was an experimental car. The wheelbase of the DB4GT is five inches shorter than the DB4 and it is 1½ cwt lighter, which helped to give the car exceptional performance, with acceleration to 60 mph in a fraction over six seconds and a top speed in excess of 150 mph.

In 1960 an even more exciting car made its appearance in the form of the Zagato-bodied DB4GT. Nineteen such cars were made and though most of them were returned to the works with the new bodyshell untrimmed, this car is one of six that was completed in Italy, its first owner's name being Zagato. It has a bonnet air vent, not usually to be found on this model.

Another Zagato dating from 1962 and a works-finished car. Its whereabouts were unknown for some years until its fairly recent reappearance. Though not in its original paint colour and with one other detail difference—the seats—it is nevertheless one of the very best examples of the type to be found.

The last but one of the DB4GT Zagatos. This was built as a left-hand drive car but was converted to right-hand drive after it arrived in this country in 1973.

In 1963 the DB4 gave way to the DB5 which was similar in many respects to the last of the DB4 cars. Its main difference was the engine which was enlarged to 3,995cc, generally known as the 4 litre. One other useful improvement was the fitting of an alternator which was better able to cope with the electrical system which featured a heated rear screen and electrically operated side windows as standard equipment, for the first time.

This is a DB5 with a difference. It has two handbrakes, but history hasn't recorded why.

One of the most famous Aston Martins of all time—the James Bond DB5, seen here undergoing maintenance between its many promotional visits. At the time this picture was taken, the film 'Goldfinger' was a fading memory but this did nothing to diminish the huge attraction that the car still held. The spare wheel, seen here on the parcel shelf, travelled wrapped in brown paper on the rear seat, since the normal spare wheel location was filled with a mass of hydraulic and electrical equipment. This is the car that set fire to the freight doors of the Boeing 707.

The control centre of the Bond car, showing the radar screen, the concealed radio telephone, the controls for the bullet-proof shield, revolving number plates and the assortment of oil and tacks that could be fired out of the rear of the car.

Defensive extending over riders and the bullet-proof shield help to protect the rear of the car.

The slicing device which made a mess of the Ford Mustang in the film Goldfinger.

One of the 125 convertible DB5 models which were built at Newport Pagnell between 1963 and 1965.

Some of the DB5 convertibles were sold with the optional hardtop.

Seen at the first Aston Martin Club visit in 1977, another of the short wheelbase Volantes, with its hood down.

Convertible versions of the DB6 were also available and this is the model with which the name Volante is usually associated. The hood is power-operated for the first time, using hydraulics fitted within the boot compartment.

With the hood raised or lowered, the Volante in either form is equally pleasing.

The only Volante to have a works-fitted hardtop, this being on a 1967 model. This modification was done at the request of the owner, a Shropshire journalist who now owns one of the two DBS two-seater prototypes.

The successor to the DB6 was nearly called the DB7 which seemed logical. However the differences were too few to justify the new title, hence the DB6 Mk 2. This car was produced with the DBS, taking over from the DB6 in 1969. It can be recognised by the flared wings, needed to accommodate larger tyres. An electronic fuel injection system was offered for the first and only time on the six-cylinder engine. Unfortunately this system never fulfilled expectations and many of the engines so fitted have since been converted to Weber carburettors.

In 1967 the Company announced the DBS, its first totally new model for almost 10 years. It represented quite a big departure from the earlier format because of the considerable increase in size. It used the same 4-litre engine that appeared originally in the DB5 though now with a higher degree of tune. This particular example is one of the best of the type to be found and 10 years after its registration it was still in the hands of its original owner.

The engine compartment of the DBS was designed for a larger power unit than the six-cylinder engine which first appeared in it. In 1969 the new DBS V8 model using an engine which had been under development for some years, including a none too successful venture to the 24-hour race at Le Mans in 1967, was revealed. In its first form the V8 was fitted with fuel injection and except for the wheels, which were light alloy instead of the steel wire type, and brakes, which were very much more powerful, and a new automatic gearbox, the car was similar in specification to the DBS which was being built at the same time.

In May 1972 the Company, now no longer a part of the David Brown Corporation, announced the Aston Martin Vantage. This model was technically similar to the earlier DBS. It used the same engine but only in the higher Vantage tune. Its production life was a little over a year during which 70 were produced. The car shown is in fact the last of those cars and the last to be made, using the well-proven six-cylinder engine.

The DB5 continued the use of this simple pinnacle arrangement which was first used in the DB Mk III.

The interior of the second DBS prototype. The instruments are fitted in a wooden panel, something not seen since the DB 2/4 Mk II.

The last version of the Aston Martin traditional wooden steering wheel which gave way to a smaller diameter leather-covered wheel, was then available as an option for a short time, before finally being dropped in 1973. The instrument size was similar to that in the DB6 but the operation of some of the smaller auxiliary ones had reverted to the sector type of the earlier DB5.

The facia layout of a 1973 V8. Though the instruments and their position are unchanged from the earlier cars the main controls have undergone some changes.

The Marek-designed six-cylinder all-alloy engine in its early 3.7-litre form. This engine is shown in standard form in a 1960 DB4. The higher performance Vantage unit is recognisable by its use of three SU carburettors.

The DB4GT version of the 3.7-litre engine. The cylinder head is fitted with twelve plugs and the three carburettors are twin-choke Webers.

The same engine, but as a 4 litre, first used in the DB5. This is the standard engine which used three SU carburettors, the Vantage using Webers, similar to those on the earlier DB4GT. The camshaft covers are now secured by pairs of bolts in place of the four single bolts on the 3.7-litre version.

The V8 engine as it has been since its conversion to carburettors in 1973. This new system greatly improved accessibility for maintenance purposes.

The V8-engined DBS was unveiled in 1969, but before that, one of the units replaced a six-cylinder engine of a customer's DBS and thus became the first-ever DBSV8 in private hands.

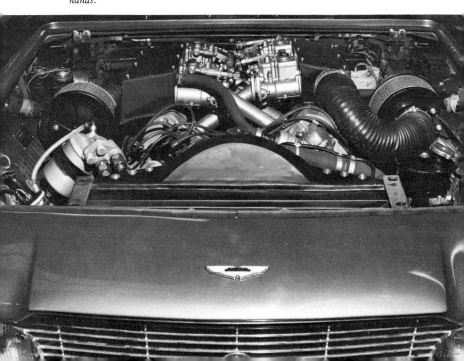

The first of the production versions of the DB3S, built betwen 1953 and 1956, on the approach to the final hairpin at Wiscombe Park.

The basic good shape of the DB4 is seen to advantage. This is a Series Two car.

Club racing, at its best. Two DB4 cars in a race-long duel at a St. John Horsfall race meeting, held each year at Silverstone by the Aston Martin Owners Club.

Another DB4GT in a hurry. There were Aston Martins in films, even before James Bond. This one featured in The Wrong Arm of the Law.

It is prudent to remove grilles and bumpers when going racing—especially when you go as fast as this DB5 is apt to do.

An early, much modified and very rapid DB4, capable of being driven fast in the wet as well as the dry.

Whereas earlier models have almost immediately found their way into competitive motoring, the DBSV8 has taken a little longer to arrive. The car shown is one of the fuel injection cars. . .

Not so with the V8 Vantage version though. Here the first production car is shown, at considerable speed, only a few months after the model's introduction.

5 Alan Curtis

Alan Curtis became managing director of one of the world's most famous and respected car companies because he happened to be in the right place at the right time. The fact that he has also proved to be the right man is a bonus, albeit a very welcome one. For fifty-one-year-old Alan, whose roots are more in property than motors, will readily admit that he was a very reluctant car boss.

His connection with Aston Martin started in 1971. At the time his new property company was going through a very successful infancy and, despite the Jaguar E-Type and Ferrari in the garage, flying was the recreational love of his life, with cars just a means of transportation. Then along came one of his two son's fifteenth birthday, and dad asked what he would like for a present. Paul didn't hesitate. 'I'd like you to buy an Aston Martin.' With young Paul being an Aston Martin nut, the answer wasn't so surprising as it may seem.

'So I bought a DBSV8,' says Alan. 'I immediately liked it—it was a man's car, but quietly unostentatious. It was an asset in my business in that I could drive it anywhere and I didn't appear to be flaunting my money.' Alan changed his Aston each year for several years, but still didn't become hooked. 'Then, one evening in 1974, I came home and Paul said he'd heard on television that Aston Martin had gone under. I was staggered, but it was hardly, at that time, an important event to me. I said: "What a shame, now let's have dinner".'

'Paul read everything he could about the company's problems, and he even stuck "Help Aston Martin" stickers on my Ferrari and E-Type. He kept urging me to try to save the firm, so eventually I called my solicitor and auditor and, early in 1975, we went to the factory to have a look round. Their subsequent report was

101

borderline—there was just enough possibilites to keep me interested.

'I came back to Newport Pagnell a couple of times, and in fact while walking round the factory on one visit I decided to show my faith in the company by ordering a car from the Receiver who was running Aston Martin while negotiations were going on with potential buyers. I remember putting a cross in the dust on the bonnet—the place, as you can imagine, was like a ghost town, with half-finished cars all over the place. I still wasn't really interested in buying the firm, although Paul kept egging me on.

'Then I heard that an American and a Canadian were interested in buying Aston Martin, and that they had formed a consortium with an Englishman. I suggested to my accountant that we should put a bid in, but he advised me to hold back as the consortium was due to sign within a few days. I was prepared to pay £650,000, but the consortium did sign and I thought: "Great, now I can forget all about it".'

The consortium, who paid £1,050,000 for the company, comprised an American, Peter Sprague, and a Canadian, George Minden. Alan was subsequently to learn that the Englishman was no longer involved. 'About six weeks later the telephone rang while I was in my bedroom, and Paul came tearing up the stairs shrieking: "Peter Sprague's on the 'phone." To him Peter, who had helped to save Aston Martin, was one removed from God. Peter introduced himself and said that he understood I had been interested in saving the company. I told him I was delighted that he had bought it, and he told me he wanted an English partner, but that he had a problem. It was then that I learned the Englishman in the consortium was no longer involved, and Peter said that Aston Martin was an English company, and without an Englishman it was a nonsense and he wouldn't go on.

'I told him I would think about it, but he persuaded me to have dinner with him at the Dorchester the following evening. As soon as I met him I was impressed by him, and I liked him. We talked about Aston Martin—Peter had owned several of the cars over the years—and the more he talked the more I became interested. We agreed to meet at the factory the following week and we walked around. It was just starting up again, and we discussed how the company should be organised and what finance would be necessary. I was quite surprised to find that we seemed to agree on everything—we were both thinking along the same lines. We had dinner at the Swan Revived in Newport Pagnell that evening and over the sweet course we shook hands—I had

103

become a shareholder in Aston Martin. The next day I arranged for money to be put in.'

That was August, 1975, and two weeks later Alan met George Minden, the other survivor of the original consortium, for the first time. 'I liked him immediately too, and thought that he showed tremendous flair for what such a car should be like.' George's knowledge, in fact, had come from years of selling expensive cars in Canada, including Aston Martin, from a Toronto dealership. 'We talked about a fourth man who had left a cheque with the Receiver in the hope of helping to save the company—we thought he just had to be worth knowing. We called him and met him some five to six weeks later. We all seemed very happy with each other, and he joined us.' So the Aston Martin Lagonda (1975) quartet of shareholders was formed—Sprague, Minden, Curtis and the latest addition, Denis Flather, a retired steel businessman.

'I did not have a directorship at that time—I had more than enough on my plate with my property company, and in addition I had also just been invited to join Telford New Town Development Corporation. Also, not long before, I had bought an airfield and was busy setting up a charter service and a flying school. But, needless to say, Paul and my other son, Nicholas, were absolutely delighted, and there is no doubt that they were the main reason for my putting money into Aston Martin. I suppose a father tries to live up to what he believes his children want of him.'

At the end of 1975 Alan became, with Denis Flather, a director of Aston Martin, but apart from board meetings his involvement with the company was minimal for several months. Early in 1976, however, discussion began on a new car which was to bring to Aston Martin unprecedented publicity, which was to be used as a vehicle to persuade the world that the company was back to stay—but which was also to bring considerable traumas and heartache.

'In February of 1976 we talked about a new car for the first time. We looked at sketches by William Towns, and we decided that this was the car we wanted—it looked absolutely right. Part of the design from Towns and our chief engineer, Michael Loasby, included the extensive use of electronics for the instrumentation and other functions and Peter, who is chairman of a semi-conductor company, immediately became interested. I was all for it too, because electronics had been used in aircraft for years.' By October of that year a prototype—called simply the Aston Martin Lagonda, the Aston

Martin name being added to Lagonda because the latter was little known outside the UK—was exhibited at Earls Court. The car, which was discussed seriously for the first time only eight months before, caused a sensation and stole the thunder from every other car at the Motor Show. Overtaken by events, the Aston Martin management made production and delivery promises which were not only unattainable, but which were to cause problems for months to come.

'Not long after the Motor Show it became apparent that we had outgrown the old management structure which we had adopted on re-forming the company, and that we needed to re-structure for the Eighties. At about this time Fred Hartley, the managing director, resigned and we thought initially of trying to buy in someone. But we didn't know where to start, in any case it would have taken a devil of a long time. So it became obvious that one of we four shareholders had to become more involved and take over. We talked about it at length. Peter was in the States, George was either in Canada or Switzerland, where he has a villa for the winter, and Denis was retired. I was the only one available, and the unanimous choice! I told the other three shareholders that I was negotiating to buy another company, but if the deal did not go through I could manage it.'

The deal didn't go through and Alan, like it or not, was appointed managing director of Aston Martin in March of 1977. 'I had to re-organise the management of my property and aviation companies to enable them to run independently of me, and quite frankly I was able in each case to get together a very good management team. I also sold off some other interests, but it all took time, and it wasn't really until the beginning of 1978 that I could consider myself the full-time managing director.'

Some frantic work was going on behind the scenes at Newport Pagnell to consolidate the position given to the newly re-formed company by the Lagonda and by the new management structure, which included making four members of the senior management associate directors—Mike Loasby (director of engineering); David Flint (director of manufacturing): Nigel Butten (director of finance), and Tony Nugent (director of sales). 'When I became managing director it was my intention to phase out the V8 because I believed it was outdated. But the response of the workforce about the quality of the car and the numbers built meant that we were able to establish ourselves in the market place and bring the price from a loss-making situation to break even and eventually into what is, now, a modest profit.'

Alan enlarges on the quality aspect, and the numbers built. 'There is no doubt that, at times after we reformed Aston Martin, the quality of the cars we built was not all it should have been. In addition we were sometimes building four a week, sometimes five and occasionally six. By the end of 1977 we were building a consistent six a week, and to a very high standard, which was enabling us to make a profit. I regard that as one of the most important features of my first year as managing director, but I didn't wave a magic wand. It was due to the response from the shop floor.'

It would hardly be an exaggeration to say that all the world's eyes were on the Aston Martin Lagonda from the moment it was unveiled to the public on the eve of the 1976 London Motor Show. It had all the necessary ingredients: a new car from a company which less than two years before was on the verge of extinction; a car which had the most advanced electronic features ever seen in a production model, all housed in one of the most striking bodies on the road; and a car handbuilt in a way which is fast disappearing. Potential customers clamoured to order one, stories were written about oil sheikhs who ordered several at a time, and within weeks the car became almost a cult figure.

The prototype shown at Earls Court was, at the time, the only one in existence, and such was the short time span between that sketch being agreed by the board to the Motor Show that it had never even been run under its own power. After the show some journalists wrote stories about the 'supercar which has never been driven'—a fact which the management had not hidden from the Press—and so Aston Martin agreed to a move which must be unique in motoring history: television cameras were invited, about a month after the show, to film the car as it was driven for the very first time out of the factory doors. It passed with flying colours, and within minutes had reached 70 mph!

The problems, however, were there, and it was Alan's job to sort them out. 'The company promised delivery dates for the Lagonda at the 1976 Motor Show which we didn't have a cat in hell's chance of keeping, and this led to all sorts of trouble with the customers, public and Press. During 1977 we went through a crucial development phase with the car, and I must confess that at times I thought we had made an appalling mess of the whole thing. We'd underestimated the time it would take to develop the car—which, after all, contained many innovations for the automotive world—and some of the costings were sheer guesswork. We made the necessary moves to bring the programme into some semblance of shape, but in my view, we only cleared the hurdle of development in March, 1978.' The first Lagonda was delivered, with great Press interest, the following month.

During 1977 a new variation of the V8 was introduced, and by being called the Vantage it resurrected a name last used four years previously. This featured an uprated engine in the familiar (ex-DBS) body and, with acceleration to 60 mph in less than 5½ seconds and to 100 mph in about 13, it was, at the time, the world's fastest accelerating production car. To many, that car is the ultimate development of the DBSV8 theme, and it restored to the name of Aston Martin the ultra high-performance image which the name's heritage conjures up.

A move actively pursued by Alan during 1977 and into 1978 illustrated how important the American market had become to the company. 'Our American distributors had been asking for a convertible version of the V8 since we bought the company, and in April 1977 I saw for myself how great the demand was when I visited the Los Angeles Motor Show. We also shipped the prototype Lagonda out there for the show, and I came back with two intentions: to get that Lagonda ready for America, but to get a convertible V8 designed and in production first. After a lot of development work the convertible was given the go-ahead early in 1978, and our distributors in the States, through our American company, ordered the first year's production.'

But what of the future for a company which is as well-known for its financial traumas as for its products? 'I have no doubt that Aston Martin is now back to stay, and that opinion is based on a variety of reasons governed by the head, not the heart. Since becoming managing director I have been able to watch closely those men on the shop floor building the car, and the pride they have in their work. Do you know it takes three months to build every single car? What we are doing here is unique, and we are providing a product which is exclusive, and there will always be a market for that. We will ensure that an Aston Martin and an Aston Martin Lagonda remains exclusive by never building more than seven a week, and we shall ensure the highest possible standards of workmanship.

'The future of this company also depends on a mixed build, and this we have at present with the V8 saloon and convertible, and the Lagonda. I believe the V8 saloon has a life, with revisions, of at least three years ahead of it, while the Lagonda has an absolute minimum, at two to three a week, of five years. As I speak, we have sold every car which we plan to build for nearly the next year, and that means we are able to plan in a way which has probably never been possible before with Aston Martin. We are also setting up a special-build department capable of building one-off motor cars for the connoisseurs of this world, we plan to expand our service department, and we have formed an electronics division which is growing into a lusty young child and will reach adulthood by about 1982. That has a great future.'

The need to reduce fuel consumption is something which is relevant even to a company like Aston Martin, although anyone who can afford at least £20,000 for a car—rising to well over £30,000 for the Lagonda—might not perhaps have to watch the pennies as much as most. 'We are always looking at ways of reducing fuel consumption, and one idea is to increase efficiency by mixing air and fuel electronically, but I think that world governments and public opinion will accept that there will always be a few, such as Aston Martin, using petrol at the rate that they do.'

Augustus Bertelli will doubtless be delighted to hear that Alan would 'dearly love' to see Aston Martin back in racing. Robin Hamilton, the company's Midlands distributor, campaigns a V8-based racer in such events as Le Mans, but Alan believes the time will come when the company is asked by a private customer to build a car exclusively for such events. 'Our name is synonymous with racing—it is a deep tradition. I also believe there is a spin-off for the manufacturer, even though the racing cars of today are so far removed from road-going vehicles. There has got to be some benefit, although regretfully we couldn't afford to run a works team, as in the past.'

With genuine conviction, the latest in a long line of Aston Martin managing directors continues: 'Myself and my fellow shareholders must realise that our greatest assets are the people we have got working with us. As Peter Sprague puts it:"We invest our money, they invest their labour". I think it is indicative of Aston Martin that, despite my initial misgivings at taking over as managing director, I am now enjoying it very much. I have never before ex-perienced anything like it—working with people who have so much quality. I enjoy just standing and watching them put those cars together. There is a satisfaction in Aston Martin that I have never felt anywhere else in business.

'If I was truthful, I should admit that, to a great extent, Aston Martin has taken over from aeroplanes as the love of my life. Aren't I lucky being able to enjoy them both, instead of just one?'

It is impossible to escape the mood of optimism now prevailing at the Aston Martin plant. Those beneath regard those at the top as sound of wind, limb, finance and business sense, while those at the top look upon those beneath as men and women of skill, dedication and loyalty. Many of them have been through hard times with Aston Martin and, if they were truthful, they'd probably admit a slight fear that those times could return. Once—or for some, twice—bitten, three times shy. Yet they also know that they are building a car which has earned its colours in a fiercely-competitive world and which is now being regarded, by some, as a classic, while beside it is a brash, bright and breezy newcomer which has taken that same world by storm.

Laced with that optimism, though, is an air of business efficiency and management expertise which might be regarded as out of place among the cottage-industry aura which permeates from the factory. But to survive into the Eighties and beyond needs that efficiency and expertise. Aston Martin's ship may have been sunk frequently with the survivors clinging to the last lifeboat, but eventually a huge wave is bound to come and swallow the lot. So doesn't it make more sense to build the ship properly in the first place?

The Aston Martin V8 in its present form, wearing the distinctive and so convenient registration number that has been used since the model's introduction in 1973.

The V8 Vantage, even more powerful than the car on which it is based: the previous Vantage models. This car was announced in February 1977 and is built only to order. At its introduction it became the world's fastest accelerating production car, reaching 60 mph from rest in less than 5.5 seconds and 100 in 13. The differences between it and the standard car are mainly in the engine unit, involving different camshafts, valves, carburettors and manifolds, modified pistons (machined to clear big inlet valves) and distributor. The rear wheels are fitted with spacers and the tyres are wider than those on the standard cars.

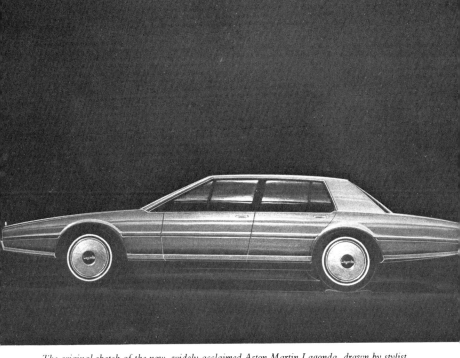

The original sketch of the new, widely-acclaimed Aston Martin Lagonda, drawn by stylist William Towns in the early part of 1976. It was sketches such as this which persuaded the Aston Martin board to develop an entirely new and innovative car.

The clay model in William Town's studio showing the final shape of the car.

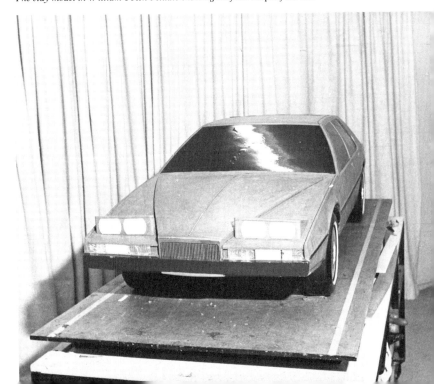

The prototype unveiled to the Press in October 1976, a week before its public debut at the London Motor Show at Earls Court. Behind the car stand the two men who together rescued the Company from almost certain oblivion and whose subsequent influence made conditions possible for this venture to be carried through. George Minden (left) is talking to Peter Sprague.

The car that was the centre of attraction at its first appearance in 1976 arrives home at Newport Pagnell after a memorable ten-day stay at Earls Court.

The instrument panel as it is today. The main instruments are now smaller and without the in-built warning lamps which are now mounted in a row at the top of the panel. The stereo-cartridge player has given way to the more compact cassette type.

A placard outside a local newspaper shop in Newport Pagnell, December 1974.

The return of the marque to Le Mans, after an absence of thirteen years. The picture shows the privately-prepared Aston Martin V8 which ran in the 24-hour race in 1977, in company with one of the turbocharged Renaults, in the first hour of the race. Only one of these two cars was running at the end of the race and it wasn't the Renault.

6 Rex Woodgate

Rex Woodgate is known as 'Mr Aston Martin' to thousands of Americans. It is a title earned not only by his flowing moustache, emphatic English speech— 'when Americans comment on my accent I tell them it's them with the accent, not me'—and his thoroughly British air, but also by his love of the marque and his utter conviction that it is second to none. He has travelled the length and breadth of the United States persuading, cajoling, praising and criticising in the cause of the boys back in little old Buckinghamshire. He has seen good times and bad, experienced highs and lows, received brickbats and bouquets, and suffered delight and heartache, during nearly a quarter of a century of service to the company.

England was brought up on a diet of craftsmen. It is the side of industry and business at which we excel, and one which is almost taken for granted. Across the cold Atlantic, however, mass-production is the compulsory menu. It is fed to the workers and consumers with ever-increasing intensity, and it is eaten with alacrity. In a country of more than 200 million people, success has to be measured by quantity rather than quality.

To an American, Aston Martin is as unbelievable as a twelfth-century church or a village pub's snug bar. Here is a motor car manufacturer who builds no more than six—yes, six—cars a week, who uses the hands of men and women to achieve it, and who has the audacity to charge more than 40,000 dollars for the privilege of owning one. Nowhere is America's amazement at Aston Martin better expressed than in a company advertisement which was run in the Wall Street Journal and other leading publications during 1977. 'In 53 years, we have produced 8,500 motor cars—about as many as roll out

of Detroit every 20 minutes,' says the ad. Such a fact smacks of British quality and sheer individualism and exclusivity. To America's credit it is the sort of thing they love, and happily for Aston Martin there are enough Americans who can afford to indulge themselves. The United States is now the company's biggest export market, and its muscle is shown by the fact that the convertible version of the V8, introduced in 1978, came into being because of pressure from Aston Martin's U.S. company, and from Rex Woodgate.

Rex was born in London in 1926, and during his early days he became interested in motor racing, with regular visits to Brooklands, Crystal Palace and Donington. The war interrupted his education at Marylebone Grammar School and, with name on his lapel, he was evacuated to Cornwall. 'There I stayed with a lovely family called Moss, but after a few months nothing seemed to be happening in London and I returned home—just in time for the war to really get going. I had always been fascinated by mechanical things, and I became an apprentice toolmaker with Smith's, the instrument manufacturers, who had a factory at Neasden.

'I was soon regarded as one of their promising pupils, and as a result they sent me down to their college in Cheltenham. Another of my interests was aeroplanes—I had always dreamed of racing one— and when my brother, who was a night fighter pilot, was killed I volunteered for the Royal Air Force. The Swiss professor who was principal at the college heard that I had volunteered and said: "How dare you volunteer when you have the opportunity to study under me". He cancelled my registration for the RAF on the grounds of essential occupation, and that was that'.

But for Rex, his disappointment at not following his beloved brother's flying footsteps was soon to be compounded by a Government move. 'Bevan came up with this scheme to recruit young men by secret ballot for working in the mines. My name came up and I found myself digging coal in South Wales in a seam less than three feet high'. Rex continued this unpalatable work as one of the renowned 'Bevan Boys' until the end of the war, when he was allowed home on medical grounds due to a knee injury caused by being buried in a fall in a mine. 'I got a job as an equipment tester at British Acoustic Films at Shepherds Bush as my father was involved with the business.' But Rex's heart was still elsewhere, and after a year he entered an arena he was to grow to love, and which was to evenually involve him with Aston Martin. 'I wanted to get involved with racing, and I went to

117

work as a mechanic with Thomson and Taylor, who built racing and world record speed cars at Brooklands. At that time I lived at Harrow, and my next-door neighbour raced cars, and I became part of that circle of people. Due to this I met Stirling Moss, and in 1949 I left Thomson and Taylor and went to work for him as a mechanic, as he was just about to start road racing. I prepared his car for the 1949 season, and then I went, again as a mechanic, to H.W.Motors of Walton-on-Thames.'

HWM were run by John Heath and George Abecassis, who were forming a Formula Two team with their own cars aimed at putting English racing back on the map. 'John, me and others designed the cars, I helped to cut the bits and pieces up, and Jack Tolley from Cooper Cars came over in the evenings and welded everything together. By the beginning of the 1950 season we had built five cars literally by hand. They were raced throughout Europe that year and, while we didn't cover ourselves with glory, we did win some races and we usually finished in the first three.' Stirling Moss—Rex's old boss— was one of the drivers, as were Peter Collins and Lance Macklin, the latter also being, with Abecassis, a works driver at the time for none other than Aston Martin.

Rex left HWM after the 1950 season and became a mechanic for two years with Gordon Watson, who was also a Formula Two racing driver, and following this he worked on a number of privately-owned cars. 'Then I joined Les Hawthorn—Mike's father—to work on the cars he prepared for private individuals, and one I particularly remember was a 2½-litre Ferrari raced by Reg Parnell in 1953. Parnell was also a works Aston driver, and he recommended me to the then competitions manager, John Wyer, as a mechanic. I had an interview at Feltham and was engaged to build production versions of the DB3S racing car.' The year was 1954, and Rex was with Aston Martin in the world of racing cars which he loved so much.

'Originally 20 production DB3S models were to be built but we finally did 19. They were mainly used by private owners for racing, but some were registered for the road and three were converted to hard-tops, one of which was used by David Brown and another was bought by the Hon. Max Aitken. At this time I was also a mechanic for the racing team and I recall that, with a lot of overtime, I made £1,000 in a year, which was a lot of money then. I thought I had really made it. I was then transferred to the service department to look after the production DB3S cars I had helped to build, and one of them was owned by Commander Arthur Bryant of the U.S. Navy, who was racing in Europe. I had to take two V12 Lagondas down in a transporter to Italy one weekend for use in a film called *Checkpoint*, and this meant I had to miss a meeting at Oulton Park. It was the first event I had missed for a considerable while, and Commander Bryant was killed at the meeting when he broke his neck in a freak accident.

'The replacement for the DB3S was the DBRI, and I was transferred back to the racing department in 1955 to work on this and then its successor, the DBR2. In 1958 I took two DBR2s to America to race at Nassau, and when the cars were shipped back to England during Christmas of the following year I and my wife decided to stay in the States. I had travelled all over the country by then and thoroughly enjoyed the happy, free way of life. I didn't have a job, but soon I joined the team of a well-known racing driver called Bob Grossman, and I prepared his Ferrari during the 1960 season. In the middle of 1961 I rejoined Aston Martin at the request of John Wyer, who was general manager by this time, and was made the factory service representative for North America, with an office at J. S. Inskip, the importer/distributor for Aston Martin in New York.'

Seeing the opportunities of selling such a quality product in the States, Rex became convinced that the company should set up its own importership rather than use a number of importers/distributors. 'I persuaded Steve Heggie, who was then managing director, that we should bring in and distribute the cars ourselves if we wanted the job done properly, and on 1 May 1964, I, as general manager, opened up Aston Martin Lagonda Incorporated at a warehouse offered to us by a friend of David Brown at King of Prussia, near Philadelphia, and we were there for 14 years.'

At the time of AML Inc's formation the DB5 was selling for 12,500 dollars, although, as Rex puts it, the States wasn't at this time taking many cars. 'Quite frankly there were certain complaints about the cars, and it was a problem setting up dealers.' But by 1967 there was considerable light at the end of the tunnel, for in that year a total of 97 DB6 models were sold and the marque's reputation was on the ascendancy. 'They were considered prestigious, high-quality cars which had a certain amount of mystique about them. We sold them on a platform of performance, quality and the racing heritage'.

The following year the company opened its own showrooms in New York's 72nd Street, and then came a bungle which was to hit Aston Martin sales in the States for a number of years. 'From 1968 the

DB6 was not certified for sale in the U.S., and so we had to rely on the six-cylinder DBS. Not long after opening the showrooms our PR in England announced the DBSV8 and sent the details to us for release to all the papers. But he hadn't indicated that it was a car for the future, and all the papers carried the story of this new V8-engined DBS. It killed sales of the six-cylinder version stone dead and gave us a really bad time. It was damned annoying. The V8 didn't arrive in the States until October 1971, and for the preceding two years we had a very thin time indeed.'

Unfortunately, however, matters hardly improved with the arrival of the DBSV8. 'From October of 1971 until the end of the year a number were imported, but the certification to sell these cars ended on 31 December, and we were without certified cars for nearly three years, until October 1974. We managed to survive on service, spares and bibs and bobs, but can you imagine trying to run a company like that? We reduced staff, and there we were in 1973 trying to sell cars which had a 1971 certification, for we weren't allowed to sell cars built after 31 December 1971. And to make matters worse, we didn't even know if we were ever going to get any more cars to sell.' Ironically, it was at the beginning of this difficult period, in 1971, that Rex was made President of AML Inc.

'Anyway, one of the Newport Pagnell staff came over in 1973 to close us down because they could not get any more cars into America. I argued the point, and said that, given 4,000 dollars and four weeks, I could produce a V8 which would meet the emission standards and thus get us certification to sell in the States. Within a few weeks I was sent an uncertified V8 and told to get on with it. By now the fuel injection had been dropped in favour of carburettors, and I took the car over to Ak Miller in Los Angeles, who was a turbocharging specialist. We fitted a turbocharger and we met the requirements— and it was within four weeks. We shipped the car back and there were plans to productionise it with a turbocharger.'

But once again fate intervened. 'When the car got back to England, Weber, who provided the carburettors, said that if the engine could meet the regulations in the States with a turbo, it could meet them without. They got to work on it, but the three-day week due to the miners' strike hit England and everything was delayed. Work was still going on early in 1974, but I said it was pointless working hard to meet the 1974 regulations and then just have a few months to sell the car, and suggested that the programme was delayed until we knew the 1975 standards and then go flat-out to meet these.

'This was agreed, and in October of 1974, after a 50,000-mile durability test during which the car was driven day and night for five months, the car was proved to meet the emission standards and we were certified for sale in the States for the first time since 1971. Between then and the end of the year 30 cars were shipped to us, and we had to set up new dealers, as we had lost nearly all of them because we didn't have any new cars to supply to them. Then, just as we were getting going again, the company back in England went bust. When the news got out we had a number of people ringing us up offering to buy for a low price the cars we had in stock—I remember one man offered us 10,000 dollars against the retail price of nearly 35,000!

'We in the States never went bust, however, and we continued doing business while trying to interest a number of people in buying the parent company. There was some interest but they were never needed, as Peter Sprague and George Minden came on the scene. I recall that Peter rang our service dealer in New York after reading an obituary on the company in the New York Times, the dealer contacted me, and I supplied Peter with all the necessary details'.

With the new owners Aston Martin became even more acutely aware of the opportunities in the States than ever, and in 1976 nearly 90 V8 models were sold just two years after sales had been nil. Then, of course, there is the convertible. 'America has always had a love affair with the convertible, but Government safety regulations killed it off. A subsequent court case decreed that the Government had acted unconstitutionally, but by then all the American manufacturers had stopped, or were about to stop, producing them. Then Jensen went out of business and with them went the Interceptor convertible, and there was a great gap. Since Peter and George took over I had been badgering Newport Pagnell to produce a convertible for the States and in 1978 they agreed. Within weeks our dealers and we ourselves had ordered the first year's production.' Deliveries of this newcomer started in the summer of 1978, although by then Rex was no longer in the States, having moved back to the factory at the beginning of that year to liaise on a variety of sales, marketing and engineering matters.

Back in England, Rex reminisces on the times, both good and bad. 'Americans feel the Aston Martin is better built and more practical than, for example, the Italian equivalent, and they also like the name of Aston Martin. But they were always hard to sell, as no one is prepared to pay out that sort of money in the States without someone working hard at it. After all, it must remembered that a V8 costs three times as much as a top Cadillac. And then there are, of course, the emission regulations, which quite frankly I feel have gone too far. It's crazy that with the emission equipment the cars consume more fuel, and America is getting concerned at the lack of fuel. It is also crazy that a private individual is legally allowed to take off the equipment once he had bought the car.'

Despite the continual struggle, however, Rex retains fond memories of the United States and its people, although one name which springs readily to mind is that of a retired British Air Force officer, Group-Captain Hugh Groves. 'He always insisted on having the first of each model brought into the States. He had a DB4, DB5, DB5 convertible, DB6, DB6 Volante, DBS and a DBSV8 before he died.' Rex smiles, and two further episodes during his twenty years in the States spring to mind. 'There was this salesman called Mike Ashley who travelled the world with the James Bond DB5. On one of his visits to the States he tried to impress journalists while at Miami, and he fired the smokescreen that was built into the car. But it backfired, and he set fire to the freight doors of the Boeing 707 in which he had arrived.

'And there was the time when I demonstrated one of the first DBSV8s to arrive in the country in 1971. I was showing off to the prospective customer the various advantages of the car and I mentioned that it had an adjustable steering column. I loosened the locking nut and to my horror the wheel came away in my hands. There we were doing about 90 mph and I was holding the wheel. Luckily it was a straight road, but since I was so embarrassed I decided to make light of it, so I handed the wheel over to the potential purchaser and asked him if he would like to take the wheel. He closed his eyes and I quickly locked the wheel back on. And yes, he did buy a car.' With so much going against him at the time, Rex undoubtedly deserved such good fortune.

Like so many before him, Rex's story with Aston Martin is one of a battle against the odds punctuated by periods of good health. Time after time he and his staff at King of Prussia received a body blow just when it seemed they had beaten the count, but each time they bounced back. That American sales are now buoyant is a credit to their dedication and sheer determination, and with a competent young businessman installed as President in Rex's footsteps at AML Inc the future, based on the V8, the convertible and the forthcoming (to the States at least) Lagonda, looks very healthy indeed. Rex has earned his laurels back in England, but I doubt if he will rest on them.

Two production DB3S models of the sort that Rex Woodgate joined the Company to help build. Although some were registered for the road, most of them were raced by their private owners.

Although it will be remembered for other things, 1974 also had its achievements and the picture records an important one, that of the successful conclusion of the 50,000-mile emission endurance run which was necessary to regain entry into the American market. It was the first time since 1971 that new Aston Martin cars could be sold there.

Two versions of the lightweight DB4GTs which were to become well known under the Essex racing stable banner. The lower picture shows one of them wearing rather heavy and non-standard flared wings which have since been reverted to standard.

7 Sid Norman

Sid Norman looks a normal sort of chap. Certainly the cut of his clothes, the expensive watch and his smart suburban office reveal him as a man of some financial substance, but outwardly he looks no different to most successful businessmen. His wife and three sons seem conventional enough too. All outstandingly pleasant and warmly welcoming.

Yet Sid is the head of a family with an obsession. An obsession which helps to knit them even tighter as a family, but one which has, in the past, caused more than a grim face and a few tears. It is called Aston Martin.

Sid, who is 44 and boss of the family food importing business, makes no apologies for his obsession. Indeed he is quite capable, if pushed, of eloquently explaining his feelings on the subject to such an admirable extent that the listener himself feels compelled at the finish to apologise for having queried Sid's beliefs. Here is a man who has no doubts that the current Aston Martin V8 is the best thing on wheels, the epitome of motoring perfection, and a suitable subject for adulation. Hearing his views explains why Aston Martin, so often against all the odds, has survived while others have perished, and his convictions show that the blood, sweat and tears shed by Augustus Bertelli, Claude Hill and their more modern counterparts were not in vain.

Sid has owned a total of seven Aston Martins—three DB6 models and four V8s, with his current V8 being painted an eye-catching red with perfectly matching cream leather trim. The longest he has kept one of them is three years, and the shortest nine months. Not that all seven have followed one another, for there has been the occasional break when a different marque has occupied the Normans' garage in Bedfordshire. One lasted six weeks while another—a Jaguar XJS— not much longer, which is rather surprising, as Sid was an avid Jaguar enthusiast until he became hooked on the cars from Newport Pagnell.

To get an insight into how anyone can come to love what is, after all, just a means of transport, it is essential to hear the man's attitude to motoring. 'I believe it is a privilege to own a car today, and as such it should be cherished and maintained to the highest possible standard.' Cherished and maintained Sid's V8 certainly is, for every week the family goes through a washing, polishing and feeding-the-leather-seats ritual which you interrupt at your peril. Tony Nugent, Aston Martin's London-based director of sales, will tell you that an ex-Sid Norman car is as perfect as the day it left the factory, adding with a twinkle: 'Perhaps even more so.' The bodywork looks as if it is has never been out in the cold or rain, the seats don't look sat upon, and the ashtrays appear never to have housed a stub. Which they probably haven't, for before stepping into the car you'll be told very gently and courteously: 'I deplore people who smoke in my car and slam the doors shut.'

Why, though, the Aston Martin? 'I believe it is the personification of engineering perfection. I like everything about the V8—in my view it is the finest car in the world. It is beautifully engineered, has excellent styling, and gives the unmistakable, but hard-to-describe, solid feel which only a car built on a chassis like this has. On top of that it has superb handling, roadholding and performance.'

The Norman telephone rings, and the eulogistic flow is temporarily halted. At the other end is Sid's accountant, who obviously wants to talk business, but he finds it difficult. As naturally as a duck takes to water, Sid steers the conversation round to—Aston Martin. The accountant is advised that a V8 must be his next car, but he mustn't increase his charges to Sid to pay for it. If anyone doubts that a satisfied customer is a firm's best salesman, he should listen to Sid Norman talking to his accountant.

Telephone conversation over, and the threads are quickly picked up. 'Yes, you could say my love of my car is an obsession, but I get sheer pleasure and enjoyment out of it. Do you know, after a long journey I pat the car's bonnet and say: "Well done". I even feel like giving it a lump of sugar. I feel a car is an extension of myself—we form a team.

'That car'—he points out of the window to the street below—

'sums up the image I would like to have. It has obvious built-in quality and good taste without being ostentatious. I have always tried, in business, to give an image of quality and of a job being well done, and the Aston fits in perfectly. It is not a prestige symbol. I'll agree there is a prestige value in owning one, but that is not my reason for having it. I am not a believer in status symbols as a way of life.'

Sid acknowledges that the car draws a lot of attention from all ages and all walks of life, while a favourite remark from young boys is: 'I say mister, where are your machine guns?'—a reference to the James Bond DB5. It also gets treated, he says, with a lot of respect, both by passers-by and other road-users.

Sid is as well known at the Aston Martin factory as the bosses, and he is intensely proud of the fact that he receives personal service which, even for Aston Martin, is a little unusual. 'I have my own personal road tester, and when I ordered my present car I was able to have a few small Sid Norman-type modifications—but then, that is another advantage of buying a car so individually and hand made as an Aston Martin. They must dread me ordering a new car—I plague the life out of them like an excited schoolboy.'

The whole family share this enthusiasm for the marque, to such an extent that the youngest son David 'cried his eyes out' when dad exchanged a V8 for another make, and refused to speak to him for weeks. 'None of us can imagine waking up on a Saturday morning and not having an Aston Martin in the garage waiting to be cleaned.'

What of the petrol consumption of the V8 which, if not heavy in relation to the performance, is still high enough to warrant justification? 'We are told that it is socially unacceptable to have a car which uses a lot of petrol, but I disagree. The amount of petrol my car and others like it use is negligible beside the amount of fuel that is continually wasted throughout the world. In addition, the extra fuel used over a year by a car which does, say 16 miles to the gallon, in comparison with a car that does 20, is very small.

'We are told we live in a free society, so provided I pay what is asked of me by that free society, I am surely entitled to spend my money on what I want'.

It is time for lunch, and Sid has invited Roger and I to join him. As we get into his Aston Martin I'm thankful I don't smoke, and I remember not to slam the door. The ignition key is turned, the car throbs into eager life, and Sid is transported into another world, a world which only the privileged few can share. 'In life people have

129

their own ideals of what is perfect in various things. To me, this Aston Martin is perfection in a motor car.

'As a well-wisher for the company I am a great believer in their future. In any case I could not see myself in any other car.'

Nor could I, Sid.

A view of one of the policing areas in July 1977 when the Owners Club came in great numbers to the factory for the first club visit.

. . . and two versions of the DB Mk III share some shade with, in the background, a DB2 convertible.

Front ends . . . .

. . . and rear ends—all of them DB2/4 or DB Mk III models, at Knebworth House.

Summary of production figures.

Model	Body types	Prod. dates	No. made
Lionel Martin 1½-litres	Various	1914-1925	63?
Bertelli			
First series	Tourer, Convertible and saloon	1927-1932	129
Second series	Tourer and saloon	1932-1933	130
Third series	Tourer and saloon	1934-1935	166
Two Litres	Tourer, Convertible and saloon	1936-1940	174
David Brown			
DB1 2 litre	Convertible	1948-1950	15
DB2 2.6 litre	Saloon and Convertible	1950-1953	409*
DB3 2.6 and 2.9 litre	Competition two-seater	1951-1953	10*
DB2/4 Mk1 2.6 and 2.9 litre	Saloon and Convertible	1953-1955	565*
DB3S 2.9 litre	Competition two-seater	1953-1956	31*
DB2/4 Mk II 2.9 litre	Saloon, Convertible and hardtop	1955-1957	199
DB Mk III 2.9 litre	Saloon, Convertible and hardtop	1957-1959	551
DB4 3.7 litre	Saloon and Convertible	1958-1963	1,110
DB4GT 3.7 litre	Standard and	1959-1961	75
	Zagato	1960-1963	19
DB5 4.0 litre	Saloon and Convertible	1963-1965	1,023
DB6 4.0 litre	Saloon	1965-1969	1,330
DB6 Mk2 4.0 litre	Saloon	1969-1970	245
Volante Convertibles 4.0 litre	Short wheelbase	1965-1966	37
	Long wheelbase	1966-1969	140
	Long wheelbase – Mk2	1969-1970	38

DBS 4.0 litre	Saloon	1967-1972	829
DBSV8 5.3 litre	Saloon	1969-1972	405
Company Developments			
Aston Martin Vantage 4.0 litre	Saloon	1972-1973	70
Aston Martin V8 5.3 litre	Saloon	1972-	1,010
Aston Martin Lagonda (1975) Ltd			
Aston Martin V8 Vantage 5.3 litre	Saloon	1977-	23
Aston Martin Lagonda 5.3 litre	Saloon	1978-	1
Aston Martin V8 5.3 litre	Volante convertible	1978-	3

Most of the Lionel Martin cars were made after 1923

*includes team competition cars